Individualized Art Energizers

for the Elementary Classroom

INDIVIDUALIZED ART ENERGIZERS FOR THE ELEMENTARY CLASSROOM

Charlene M. Barton

Parker Publishing Company, Inc. West Nyack, NY

©1979, by

PARKER PUBLISHING COMPANY, INC.
West Nyack, N.Y.

*All rights reserved. No part of this
book may be reproduced in any form or
by any means, without permission in
writing from the publisher.*

Library of Congress Cataloging in Publication Data

Barton, Charlene M
    Individualized art energizers for the
elementary classroom.

    Includes index.
    1. Art—Study and teaching (Elementary)—United
States. 2. Individualized instruction.
3. Project method in teaching. I. Title.
N362.B37   372.5'044   79-16058
ISBN 0-13-457200-9

Printed in the United States of America

A Word from the Author

I believe that this book can help enliven your classroom, both artistically and academically! The individualized art lessons which follow will benefit each child, regardless of age or ability. There is an increased emphasis on individualized learning in education today. Because of this, you will find these projects especially appropriate as they work to release the creative energy of individuals in your class!

Most teachers agree that elementary art instruction is valuable because it helps children develop an appreciation of beauty, learn how to use various art media, and become more aware of their environment and their own relationship to it. Teachers have also discovered that art can provide a welcome change in routine and allow a child with academic difficulty another chance to succeed and gain a sense of self-worth.

The value of art instruction to other areas of learning is sometimes not fully appreciated, however. For example, good art activity promotes certain accomplishments in children which are necessary to school success. Among these are the ability to form concepts, the ability to translate information received through the eyes and ears into symbols, and the ability to put things into proper order. Furthermore, reading and writing skills benefit from the coordination of eye and hand and the fine motor coordination learned in art projects. Art lessons can also foster retention of what is learned in other subjects and can encourage a creative, imaginative approach to problem solving.

Each of the following lessons develop specific skills which are listed at the beginning. Thus you can choose which will be especially helpful to particular students. Every lesson is presented as a challenge to individuals in your class. Each will be "energized" as his interest is aroused, and he accepts the challenge! Also in every lesson you will find suggestions for using student ideas as "energizers" in motivating the class. And because each child is unique, ways of reaching every individual in your class have been included, along with hints on how to help a child appreciate his own work, as well as that of others. Methods of evaluating success conclude each lesson.

The first part of the book is devoted to carefully planned activities designed to build the skills in drawing, painting, and use of other media which each student needs to approach art as an individual. The second part contains projects that introduce your children to the fantastic worlds of their own imaginations and explore the wonders of the real world around them.

Using these lessons with boys and girls has been a very special experience for me as an art supervisor. I am grateful for all that I have learned from these children and their teachers. It is with them in mind that I have written this book, hoping that it will, in turn, be useful to other teachers wishing to bring the best possible experiences to their students.

Charlene M. Barton

ACKNOWLEDGEMENT

I would like to thank both my own children and my students for help with the many illustrations.

Also, Ernest Rose for help with the photography.

Contents

A Word from the Author 5

PART I: Basic Art Skills as Energizers 13

Chapter One: Discovering the Delight of Drawing 15

    Contour Drawing • 15
    Drawing Round Objects • 17
    Detail Line Drawings • 19
    Figure Drawing • 20
    Gesture Drawing • 22
    Texture Drawings • 24
    Still Life Drawing • 26
    Continuous Line Drawings • 28

Chapter Two: Pursuing Self Expression Through Painting 31

    Take a Deep Breath (blowing tempera paint) • 31
    Let's Get It Straight (stick painting) • 33
    Light and Bright (sponge painting)• 35
    More from Four (color mixing) • 37
    Bright, Brave, and Bold (painting with large
       brushes) • 38
    What's Important to Me (emphasizing detail) • 40
    Pleased to Meet You (portraits) • 42

Chapter Three: Tackling Techniques in Printmaking 45

Leaf Prints • 45
Potato Prints • 47
Seasonal Styrofoam Prints • 50
Christmas Cards from Oak Tag and String • 52
Oaktag Prints • 54
Stencil Silhouette Prints • 56
Tissue Paper Prints • 58

Chapter Four: Solving Problems in Sculpture 61

Scrapwood Animals • 61
Papier-Mâché Character Heads • 63
Paper-Mâché Bottle People • 65
Light Bulb Birds • 68
Foil and Cardboard Reliefs • 70
Cardboard Carton Creatures • 72
Foil Figures • 74
Totem Poles • 76

Chapter Five: Exploring the Possibilities of Paper 79

Torn Paper Scenes • 79
Indian Shields • 81
Motion Montages • 83
Creating Depth with Size and Color • 85
Wallpaper Still Lifes • 87
Designs with Repeated Shapes • 89
Transparent Tissue Windows • 90
Newspaper Compositions • 93

Chapter Six: Interpreting the World with Watercolor 97

Watercolor Wash: A Special Sky • 97
Wax Resist Paintings: Out at Night • 100
Stained Glass Windows • 101
Watercolor Portraits: Storybook People • 105
Working on Wet Paper: A Rain Forest • 107
Painting from Life with Watercolors • 110

Keeping Up the Good Work of Building Art Skills 113

Contents

PART II: Imagination and Environment as Energizers......117

Chapter Seven: Creative Play and Dramatics with Puppets..119

Paper Bag Puppet Pals • 119
Stocking Hand Puppets • 121
Papier-Mâché and Cloth Hand Puppets • 124
Stuffed Storybook Puppets • 126
Clay, Cloth, and Popsicle Stick Puppets • 128
Folded Paper Creatures • 130
Sawdust Finger Puppets • 132

Chapter Eight: Mask Making Magic 135

Paper Plate Masks • 135
Paper Bag Masks • 137
Cylinder Masks • 139
Primitive Masks of Papier-Mâché • 141
Circus Masks: Papier-Mâché over Balloons • 144
Collage Visages: Faces with Feeling • 146

Chapter Nine: Discovering Whole New Worlds 149

Huge Cut Paper Animals • 149
Shapes as Starters • 151
What Comes from an Egg? • 152
A Distant Planet • 154
Absurd Montages • 156
Cloth and Crayon Creatures • 158
Inventions That Should Be Invented • 159
Crayon and Fingerpaint: Undersea
    Excursions • 161

Chapter Ten: Individualized Awareness Activities..............165

Cut Paper Fish • 165
Self-Portraits • 167
Patterns Found in Nature • 168
Center Designs in Nature • 170
Happy Faces • 171
Aquarium Wax Resist Pictures • 173

Painting a Pet • 174
Detail Drawings of the Room • 176
Scrapwood Surprises • 177

Chapter Eleven: Mini-Excursions as Energizers 181

Wonderful Weeds • 181
Sounds While Sitting Still • 183
Looking at the Wind • 184
Texture Rubbings • 186
Package Design • 188
Getting to Know a Tree • 190
Studying Shadows • 192
Our Neighborhood Mural • 194

Chapter Twelve: Describing Experiences Visually 197

A Very Bad Blizzard • 197
A Big Yellow Bus Ride • 199
Bright Lights at Night • 201
My Room • 203
A Terrific Taste • 204
A Happy Crowd • 206
Going Fast • 208
A Sudden Shower • 209

**Keeping Up the Good Work with Imagination
and Environment as Energizers 213**

Index 217

PART 1

Basic Art Skills as Energizers

In order to use art as a means of expression, an individual child must discover how to use art materials. Part I contains a chapter on each of six media suitable for elementary students and available at most schools. You can use the individualized lessons in those chapters to help each of your students learn what he needs to know to work independently and confidently as an artist.

Drawing is an ideal activity since it requires few materials and children already know how to use most drawing tools. It is an ideal quiet, individual activity. Tempera painting is an opportunity to make bright visual statements and discover more about color. To children, who delight in making large or three-dimensional objects, sculpture is always a pleasure. Not only are the processes fun, but they also teach a great deal about balance and shape. Cut paper is an excellent way to teach children to compose pictures effectively, as well as being great for fine motor control. Students are energized by print making because they enjoy discovering ways of making more than *one* of a particular picture or design. Basic watercolor techniques are presented which help students take a free approach to painting. All the lessons are individualized and allow for the widest possible range of abilities.

The child gains more than a knowledge of art processes from Part I. In addition to discovering what he *can* do with particular materials, he learns what he *can't* do! For example, it is common for a child to seek out the tiniest brush possible in an attempt to use watercolor like a pencil. This is needlessly frustrating. Exposure to a variety of media enables him to select the material required to achieve the desired effect. He acquires an art vocabulary necessary to a discussion of art, and he grows artistically as he learns to accept a variety of styles including his own. Finally, he is introduced to the elements of art; color, texture, volume, line, and shape.

Chapter 1

Discovering the Delight of Drawing

CONTOUR DRAWING

Materials needed: 12 × 18" manila or white drawing paper, felt tip markers, oil pastels or crayons, and several plants. (See Figure 1-1.)

This activity provides practice in fine motor coordination, eye-hand coordination, generalization, organization, and translation.

Present the challenge by having students group their desks so that each student is able to closely examine one of the plants. "Today we are going to look at a plant in a special way. We are going to learn about the word 'contour,' then study a plant in order to do a contour drawing of its leaves."

Use student ideas as energizers by asking what "contour" means. Be sure that everyone understands that the contour of an object is its shape. Explain that shape is very important because often it alone can tell us what an object is. For example, without seeing color or any detail, we can recognize a shoe or

Figure 1-1
Contour Drawing

a pear just from its contour, and we can identify a tree by the shape of its leaves. Ask students to think of other things with unique contours.

Reach every individual by having each one look carefully at the plant nearest him. Say that markers will be used to draw the shape, or outside edge, of all parts of the plant. The hesitant child may be confused by so many edges. Let him draw one branch of the plant. Another child may need you to help him "see" the leaves more clearly. Focus his thinking by having him describe the shape of a leaf and whether its edges are smooth or rough. "Now try drawing one leaf. Good! Are you ready to draw more?" Some students will complain that markers can't be erased. "That's one of the reasons we are using markers. We mustn't waste time erasing. One line can't spoil a picture!"

Discovering the Delight of Drawing　　　　　　　　　　　　　　**17**

Appreciate each person as color is added to the drawings. You will find that some children will use color realistically, while others will choose colors brighter than nature. Praise each interpretation and be sure that students see that variety is a positive and desirable result.

Contour drawing is a success if an understanding of the term "contour" is gained. Have children look for contours to draw at home. If they bring in drawings, you have succeeded in capturing their interest. Related "energizers" include repeated cut paper shapes, Chapter 5, and chalk and stencil pictures, Chapter 16.

DRAWING ROUND OBJECTS

Materials needed: 12 × 18" manila paper or newsprint, charcoal, and a number of round or cylindrical objects arranged in a pleasing manner where students can see them. (See Figure 1-2.)

This activity provides practice in fine motor coordination, eye-hand coordination, generalization, and translation.

Present the challenge by showing your students how versatile charcoal can be. Tape a large piece of paper to the chalkboard. Draw a fine, light line, then a dark, thick one. Use the edge of the charcoal to make a wide shaded area. Erase the light line by rubbing it with your finger. Explain that charcoal is fun to use because one can achieve very fine lines which can be rubbed away, as well as heavy lines and shading. Tell students to use it just as it is picked up from the desk—between thumb and all four fingers, not like a pencil.

Use student ideas as energizers by drawing a circle on the board and, holding the charcoal on its side, lightly shade around the edge of the circle. Ask the children what has happened. "Right! It does look round. Does anyone know why?" Hold an orange up. "What part of this orange is the brightest? Sure, the part closest to you. It's darker where it curves away from you. If you squint your eyes as you look, you will see one spot that is brightest of all. That's called the **highlight!**"

Reach every individual by looking at the bottles, oranges, and other round and cylindrical objects with the children, encouraging them to be observant. "Notice where the bottle meets the table. What kind of line do you see there? Yes, a

Figure 1-2

curve." And, "How do you show in a drawing that some things are in front of others? Overlapping! That's the idea!" Remind them to shade the objects along the sides. Highlights can be added with white chalk last of all.

Appreciate each person as students begin drawing. You may need to show a youngster that a short piece of charcoal is easier to use than a long one. Another may ask to draw only one object. That is fine with you. Some children can "see" their work better if you hold it up some distance away. This shows them that you appreciate their pictures and helps them to do the same.

Drawing round objects is a success if your students hold the charcoal correctly and use both the end and the side in their drawings. You have succeeded in explaining the concept if most students are able to highlight the objects with chalk. Older elementary students find this lesson challenging. The younger child may not achieve a three-dimensional effect but will think the activity "grown-up" and benefit from being introduced to the idea of drawing round objects.

Discovering the Delight of Drawing 19

DETAIL LINE DRAWINGS

Materials needed: 12 × 18″ manila or white drawing paper, pens, and about three objects with interesting details which would appeal to your students—musical instruments, for example. (See Figure 1-3.)

This activity provides practice in fine motor coordination, eye-hand coordination, generalization, and translation.

Present the challenge by asking what details are. Hold up the objects that you have selected so that your students can get a good look at each one. "What are some of the details that you notice? Today we are going to do detail drawing. We must see all the details well in order to draw them!"

Use student ideas as energizers as you talk about the objects with the children. They will be anxious to share their observations. Doing so will be encouragement to really pay attention to detail.

Reach every individual as you give each child pen and paper and explain the process. Place the objects where they can be eas-

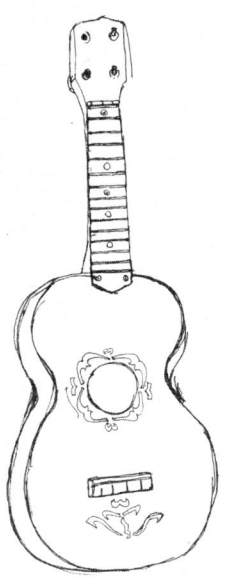

Figure 1-3

ily seen by everyone. "We are using pens today because they have a fine point and are good for drawing small parts of things. Pen and ink drawings also show up well. I know that we can't erase, but that can be a good thing. Sometimes we spend too much time erasing! Let's draw these objects as we see them and include as much detail as possible."

Appreciate each person as drawings are started. The student who makes his drawing fill the paper is off to a good start. He will have plenty of room for detail. Show others in the class. It will "energize" them to successfully approach their drawings. There is something unique and fine in every picture—a detail unnoticed by most, an interesting placement of objects, an unusually good drawing. Compliment each child. As their confidence increases, so will their eagerness to draw.

Detail drawings are successful if students are able to see and draw most of the objects' details. Ask those who are interested to remove a shoe and do a detail drawing of it in their spare time. If quite a few of your students give it a try, they have been "energized." Another related activity is detail drawing of the room, Chapter 12.

FIGURE DRAWING

Materials needed: 12 × 18" manila or colored construction paper, crayons or oil pastels. A large hat, a vest, jacket, or shawl, and perhaps a long skirt add fun and interest to this project. (See Figure 1-4A.)

This activity provides practice in fine motor coordination, eye-hand coordination, generalization, and translation.

Present the challenge by choosing a student to put on the "costume." Have him stand on a table so that he may be seen by all his classmates. He should place his feet apart and his hands on his hips.

Use student ideas as energizers by asking the children if they can see any shapes as they look at the model. "Yes, his arms do form triangles because his hands are on his hips. Sure! His legs form another triangle with the table." A hat such as a sombrero becomes yet another triangle.

Reach every individual by explaining the project so that each child becomes confident of success. Figure drawing seems formidable to a few persons in almost every class. Remind your students that thinking in terms of triangles will make their

Discovering the Delight of Drawing   **21**

Figure 1-4A

task easier. Furthermore, they need not draw the features of the face. A large hat which hides the model's face will help the children to focus on the figure rather than facial details. Older students might find it helpful if you mention something about proportion (See Figure 1-4B.)

> The head of an adult
> is about one-fifth of
> his total body length.

Appreciate each person by moving around the room and encouraging every child as he works. One may be doing a fine job capturing the "gesture" of the figure. Repeating this word will help the class remember it and relate figure drawing to gesture drawing. Perhaps one student has succeeded in showing the textures of the model's clothing. Another may be making effective use of color. These achievements shared with the class become "energizers."

Figure drawing is a success if your students complete their drawings with a minimum of direction from you and have had fun

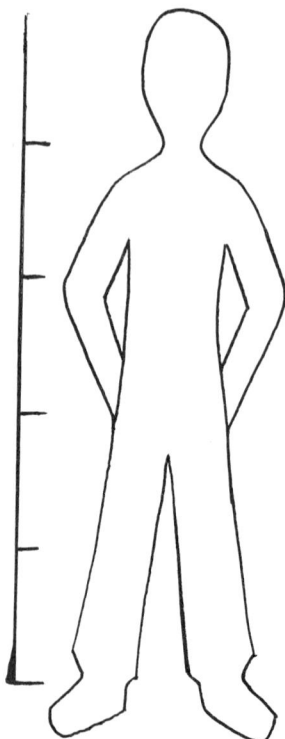

Figure 1-4B
Figure Drawing

doing it. Their confidence and pleasure reflect an adequate explanation and ample encouragement from an enthusiastic teacher. Related activities include gesture drawing in this chapter and foil figures in Chapter 12.

GESTURE DRAWING

Materials needed: 18 × 24" newsprint, black tempera paint, containers, and easel brushes. "Props" such as a step ladder, broom, jump rope, or ball are helpful, too. (See Figure 1-5.)

This activity provides practice in visual memory, translations, fine motor coordination, and eye-hand coordination.

Present the challenge by asking what happens to a football player's body when he kicks the ball. The children will probably try to answer the question by demonstration rather than explana-

Discovering the Delight of Drawing 23

Figure 1-5
Gesture Drawing

tion. "That's right. It's easier to describe action by showing it than by telling about it. Do you think that you can describe action by drawing?" Add that a motion or position is called a "gesture." Thus, sketches of action are "gesture drawings."
Use student ideas as energizers by asking a child to pretend that he is kicking a football. Urge the others to watch his movements carefully and talk about what they notice. "Sure, the football player's foot goes in the air when he kicks the ball, but what else happens? Right! Both knees bend and he rises on one toe." Someone will observe that the back and head bend as well and the arms move, too. Be sure that your students understand that the whole body is affected by a strenuous action. Explain that gesture drawings show the position of the major bones of the body. The sketches will resemble stick people. Add one more energizer. "What bones are especially

24 Basic Art Skills as Energizers

helpful to us when we move? Yes, elbows, knees, hips, and other joints. Let's show these in our sketches."

Reach every individual by giving each one several sheets of newsprint, paint, and a brush. Felt tip markers may be used if you prefer. Allow several students to take turns demonstrating an action of their choice. They may use a ball, jump rope, or other "prop" if they wish. Provide a space in the room for this purpose. Be sure that the children understand that they are making action sketches—not pictures. Do a stick-man style action sketch on the chalkboard for them to see.

Appreciate each person as students begin their gesture drawings. Although the model repeats his movements several times, he does it quickly. "You are doing very well to sketch so fast with your brush!" you tell one child. Another student has made one sketch after another until the paper is filled. "Very good! You have the right idea!" You will discover that some children are critical of their efforts and need extra encouragement in accepting their "stick-man" sketches.

Gesture drawing is a success if students are able to grasp the idea of sketching quickly with a paint brush. If most of them show motion in the figures they have painted, that's even better! Related activities could include figure drawing in this chapter and foil figures in Chapter 4.

TEXTURE DRAWINGS

The materials needed are up to you! Pens or markers will do fine, but crayons or oil pastels may be used. Also, you need 12 × 18″ paper—white drawing, manila, or colored construction. (See Figure 1-6.)

This activity provides practice in fine motor coordination, eye-hand coordination, organization, and integration.

Present the challenge by asking students if they remember touching something that really made an impression on them. "Perhaps you remember it because it felt so good. Or perhaps it is unforgettable because it felt so bad!" Ask them if they know the word for the way that things feel. "Texture. Do you think that you can show how something feels by drawing it?"

Use student ideas as energizers by having children share their memorable experiences with textures. These are likely to include touching a baby chick, a kitten, velvet curtains, or silk.

Discovering the Delight of Drawing 25

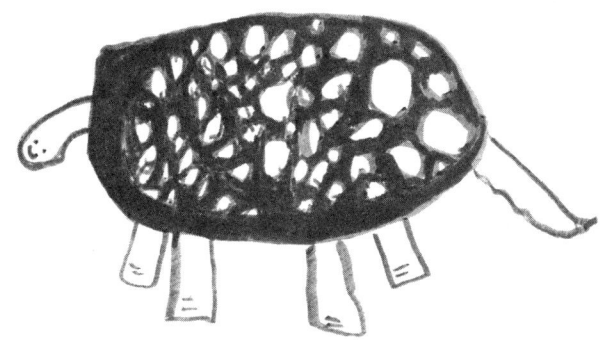

Figure 1-6
Texture Drawing

Unpleasant textures might be fingernails on a chalkboard, cold oatmeal, or even the sidewalk if you fall. Encourage students to explore the concept of texture some more. Ask for additional examples—for instance, rough like a cat's tongue or a doormat, smooth like a beach stone or marble, bumpy like a frog or tree bark. "Now let's make a picture of something we touched that had a texture which we won't forget. See if you can show how it felt by drawing it."

Reach every individual by allowing each student to choose which media would be the best for illustrating his memorable texture. Be sure that each child has an idea to work on. If a student has none, help him quickly review some of the ideas from the discussion. Avoid a situation where everyone draws chicks or kittens.

Appreciate each person as the students go to work. Some youngsters will think of an idea not mentioned. Another will find an effective way of creating the illusion of texture in his drawing. One may have chosen a media particularly appropriate to the object in his picture. Compliment them all and share their accomplishments with the whole class.

Texture drawings are a success if your students come up with drawings of creatures or things with distinctive textures. It could be difficult for some children to actually achieve a textured effect. That's to be expected. The important thing is that each child becomes more aware of textures, learning that tactile qualities can be shown in drawing. Try displaying the drawings and discussing which ones really give the impression of texture and why. This can be an additional learning experience. Related projects are texture rubbings, Chapter 11.

STILL LIFE DRAWING

Materials needed: 12 × 18" colored construction paper, crayons or oil pastels, and still life objects of assorted sizes and shapes. These could include a plant, a bowl of fruit, candlesticks, and an interesting bottle or two. (See Figure 1-7.)

This activity provides practice in fine motor coordination, eye-hand coordination, generalization, and translation.

Figure 1-7
Still Life Drawing

Present the challenge by proposing that the classroom become a "studio" and each student an artist. Explain that an artist develops his ability by drawing things that he sees. "That is called 'drawing from life.' An arrangement like this is called a

Discovering the Delight of Drawing

'still life.' Artists do still life drawings for practice or to prepare for painting. It's easier to draw an object correctly if we can look at it while we work!"

Use student ideas as energizers by asking what shapes are seen in the still life. "That's right! The plant pot is almost a rectangle and the leaves are each like a triangle. Of course the orange is round." The children will notice other objects which have almost geometric shapes. Also, encourage them to discuss the objects which are irregular in shape.

Reach every individual by asking each one to think about which objects he would like to include in his still life drawing. Point out that an artist is not a camera. Each artist may decide what to draw and what to omit. The artist may also use colors in his drawing that are not seen in the actual still life arrangement. Remind the students that some objects have been intentionally placed in front of others and suggest that they overlap some of the objects as they draw them. If students pretend that the lower edge of their drawing paper is the edge of the table closest to them, it will help them (1) to concentrate on the still life objects, and (2) make larger drawings. Let each student select his paper and suggest that he draw with a crayon or oil pastel of the same color. In this way children approach drawing more freely, since errors aren't obvious. Other colors are added when the drawing is done.

Appreciate each person as the "artists" go to work. At least one student in every group is likely to be confused at the prospect of drawing several objects, preferring to draw just one. Another child may have drawn very large objects. "See how part of this picture goes right off the paper? That can make a drawing more interesting." Show the child who works small how to cut his paper to complement his composition. If the child is drawing small because of lack of confidence, however, urge him to work larger.

Still life drawings are successful if all your students do a drawing and are generally pleased with their efforts. Congratulate yourself if many students are able to see and draw some of the shapes in the still life, overlapping an object or two. Ask how many would like to be artists again. If most hands go up, it is a rewarding learning experience. Related activities are wallpaper still life, Chapter 5 and still life of favorite things, Chapter 6, as well as the life drawing activities in this chapter.

CONTINUOUS LINE DRAWINGS

Materials needed: felt tip markers, crayons or oil pastels, and 12 × 18″ manila paper.

This activity provides practice in fine motor coordination, eye-hand coordination, generalization, and translation.

Present the challenge by "energizing" your students to think about line. "We've learned a lot about what lines can do. They can define the outside edge or contour of something, they can describe all the details of an object, and they can show how the object feels or what its texture is. Today we are going to use our imaginations and discover how long a line can be. Do you think that you could draw a fantastic fish with just one line?"

Use student ideas as energizers by asking what are some of the details of a fish which will have to be included in their drawings. Students will quickly answer fins, tails, eyes, gills, and scales.

Reach every individual by showing how just one line can include all those details. "Let's start by making a large fish shape with our markers. We can hold the paper the wide way and make our fish stretch across it from one side to the other, then back. Now, without lifting the marker from the paper, let's draw all the details. We call this a continuous line, obviously because it doesn't stop!" The fish become more fantastic as students color in all the shapes that one continuous line created. (See Figures 1-8A and 1-8B.)

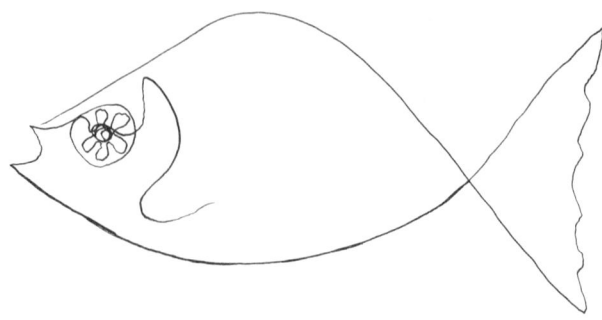

Figure 1-8A
Continuous Line Drawing

Discovering the Delight of Drawing

Figure 1-8B
Continuous Line Drawing

Appreciate each person as your students stretch their lines back and forth across the paper. You can continue teaching by using more student ideas as youngsters color their creations. "Here is a fancy fish! Almost every color is being used. This one is very interesting, too. It's all green, but see how many different shades were used!"

Continuous line drawings are a success if each child produces a "fantastic fish." You have "energized" your students in discovering more about drawing if the discussion reveals that they are learning what can be done with lines. Have every student name his fish and display them all. Then it can really be seen what kind of fish are "caught" with a long line!

Chapter 2

Pursuing Self-Expression through Painting

TAKE A DEEP BREATH
(blowing tempera paint)

Materials needed: 12 × 18″ white drawing paper, black tempera paint, straws, colored paper, cloth scraps, and glue. (See Figure 2-1.)

This acticity provides practice in fine motor coordination, translation, auditory decoding, and generalization.

Present the challenge as you suggest to your students that it could be exciting to experiment with a whole new way of using tempera paint. Show them how to drop a teaspoon of black tempera paint near the center of the bottom edge of a sheet of white drawing paper. You may need to dilute some temperas with a little water. The paint would be quite runny, yet thick enough to control.

Use student ideas as energizers by continuing the demonstration. "Do you suppose that I could use this straw to move the paint without touching it to the paper? Yes, we might be able to

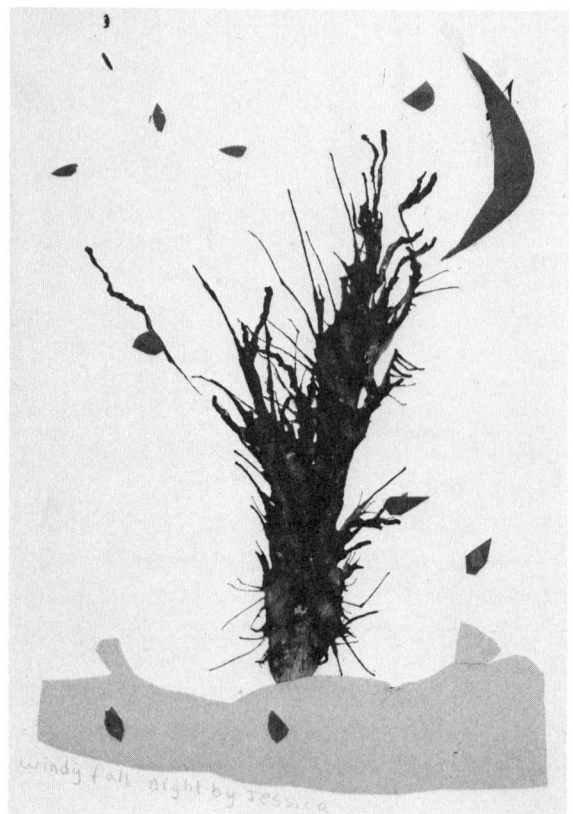

Figure 2-1
Blown Tempera

blow the paint." Explain that one should not blow directly down on the paint. It would go in all directions. "How can we get behind the paint with our breath? Sure! We can kneel on the floor by the desk. Then the straw will be nearly horizontal. Take a deep breath and blow!"

Reach every individual and show the children how to push the paint up the paper and chase each separate bead until it disappears by blowing through a straw. "Did you say that this looks like a tree? I think so, too. Perhaps it is because we made it "grow" just like a tree grows, in short, twisted spurts towards the sun! What type of a tree would you like to make from your blown tempera trunk?" Let the children discuss different kinds of fruit and flowering trees. Show them cloth

Pursuing Self-Expression through Painting 33

and paper scraps that could be used for colorful details. Suggest that each one pick up a piece of drawing paper and a straw as he returns to his seat.

Appreciate each person as you spoon the paint onto every paper. Ask what type tree the student is going to make. Be sure that everyone has an idea. As work progresses, compliment originality. "Those tissue paper scraps do make good leaves! Using those red polka dots for apples is very effective! Drawing that swing under the tree is a terrific idea!"

Taking a deep breath is a success if the students show they can blow paint gently and imaginatively. As the finished products are displayed in your classroom, point out that although all of the tempera trees were "blown," each is unique. This activity could be an energizer to start children drawing live trees outside. Have each child sketch one tree with a black marker.

LET'S GET IT STRAIGHT
(stick painting)

Materials needed: 12 × 18" colored construction paper, Popsicle sticks, styrofoam meat or produce trays, tempera paints in two colors, and newspaper to cover the desks. (See Figure 2-2A.)

This activity provides practice in fine motor coordination, eye-hand coordination, translation, organization, and generalization.

Present the challenge by asking students if they think that it would be possible to use Popsicle sticks instead of brushes as painting tools. Pour a bit of tempera paint into a styrofoam tray—not too deep, since only one edge of the Popsicle stick should be covered with paint. Show students how to press the Popsicle stick into the paint, then onto the paper.

Use student ideas as energizers while you "get into" the project. "What kinds of things do you think you could make with a straight line like this?" Trees, houses, or fences are likely to be among the initial thoughts. "How could we make a round object with this method? It doesn't work well to dip the end of the stick in the paint and use it like a pen!"

Reach every individual by inviting students to group around you. Encourage some of those who have ideas to demonstrate them for their classmates. "He's found a good way to make a circle. He kept the end of the stick in one place while he

Figure 2-2A

rotated it and pressed it repeatedly in a circle. Yes, it does look like a windmill—or maybe a dandelion." Another child will discover that printing the stick many times in a circle can suggest a round shape. And someone may find that scraping the paint along the paper is a good way to achieve a broad area of color. Urge them to discover more. "How would it look if we printed some contrasting lines over this area of color?" (See Figure 2-2B.)

Appreciate each person as you help him prepare to "get it straight." Desks should be covered with newspaper and grouped for sharing of materials. Each group should have two colors of tempera in trays; each child should have construction paper for the background, two Popsicle sticks, and a paper

Pursuing Self-Expression through Painting

Figure 2-2B
Stick Painting

towel. When the pictures are completed and left to dry, the newspaper can be wrapped around the sticks and trays and towels thrown away. It's easier to appreciate the results if clean-up has been easy!

"Getting it straight" is a success if most students are able to express a personal idea with paint and sticks. Painting is always exciting, and it is especially fun to try a new method. The sharing of several materials and your organization of the project give the children a pleasant art experience. Congratulations!

LIGHT AND BRIGHT
(tempera and sponge)

Materials needed: 12 × 18" background paper—white or colored (older students might enjoy working on 18 × 24" paper), styrofoam meat or produce trays, light blue tempera paint, crayons, and sponges cut into 2" cubes and dampened. (See Figure 2-3.)

This activity provides practice in translation, organization, generalization, and integration.

Figure 2-3
Tempera and Sponge

Present the challenge by asking students if they would enjoy trying to use a sponge as a painting tool. Show them how a dampened sponge square can be pressed into a tray of light blue paint, then gently pressed onto the paper. "You can press the sponge several times on the paper without needing more paint," you point out. "We don't want to 'scrub' with the sponge. We are painting, not cleaning."

Use student ideas as energizers as you help the youngsters approach the project. "Notice how the sponge gives the blue paint a special texture as we press it on the paper. It looks light and airy, doesn't it? It could be a good way to paint a sky." Ask your students what they would like to do if they were under such a bright blue sky. This art activity gives children a chance to make a personal expression about a pleasant sunny day experience, and it is adaptable to any season of the year.

Reach every individual as you help your class get to work. Covering desks with newspaper and grouping them to share materials make the project go more smoothly. "We will use our crayons to show what we would like to be doing on a bright blue day. The sky will be painted last of all." As the children work, you can distribute materials—several damp sponges

Pursuing Self-Expression through Painting 37

and a tray of paint for each group. This gives you a chance to see that each student has an idea to work on and is off to a good start.

Appreciate each person and his special approach to the project. Great beginnings can be shared with the class. "This picture will be a success because the crayon drawing takes up the whole lower half of the paper. The blue sky should complement our picture, not take up most of the space." Some children, in eagerness to use the paint, will be tempted to leave crayon work incomplete. "You have such a good idea! Let's be patient and put it down clearly. The paint will wait."

Sponge painting is a success if the class enjoys the effect of the light blue skies added to the bright crayon drawings. After putting the sponges in the sink and wrapping the trays in the newspaper to throw away, clean-up is complete. The airy pictures will brighten your room—and spirits—on the greyest day!

MORE FROM FOUR
(color mixing)

Materials needed: red, yellow, blue, and white tempera paints, egg cartons, newspapers, plastic spoons or tongue depressors, 12 × 18" manila paper, and crayons. (See Figure 2-4.)

Figure 2-4
Color Mixing

This activity provides practice in auditory decoding, visual memory, inference, generalization, and integration.

Present the challenge as you show your students three jars of paint—red, yellow, and blue. "How many colors do I have here?" Some child will call out the obvious answer. "Is there any way that I can get green or purple from these colors?"

Use student ideas as energizers as the children respond to your challenge. "Mix some colors together," comes the reply. Fold the 12 × 18" paper in two and place 1/2 a teaspoon of red and 1/2 a teaspoon of yellow paint near the center, refolding the paper. "What color will this combination make? Right! Orange." Gently rub the paper from the folded edge towards the outside edge, pushing the two colors of paint together and spreading them out from the center.

Reach every individual as you open the paper to admire the results. There will be exclamations of pleasure and surprise at the burst of color. Point out how many tones of red, orange, and yellow have appeared. "What does this suggest to you? A flower? A sunset? A lion? You will have a chance to mix some colors yourself when you return to your desk. Then you can turn your experiment into a picture by adding details with a crayon when the paint is dry," you explain. Try a few other combinations with your group of artists before they take their seats. Point out that red, blue, and yellow are called **primary colors.** Primary means first. These are the first colors needed to make many more. Adding white will make the colors a lighter shade.

Appreciate each person by making materials available to all. Newspaper covered desks are grouped for sharing. The four colors of paint, in an egg carton, and spoons or tongue depressors are at the center of each work area.

Color mixing is a success if everyone uses crayons over the dry paint with imagination to furnish finishing touches, turning the sprays of color into fantastic creations. Your students are learning a lot about color! Often a new approach to painting functions well as an energizer. Can each child think of a title for his picture?

BRIGHT, BRAVE, AND BOLD
(painting with large brushes)

Materials needed: 12 × 18" manila paper, large 3/4" easel brushes, egg cartons, paper towels, newspaper, and tempera paints in assorted colors. (See Figure 2-5.)

Pursuing Self-Expression through Painting 39

Figure 2-5
Large Brushes

This activity provides practice in fine motor coordination, eye-hand coordination, translation, organization, and generalization.

Present the challenge by holding up a couple of jars of tempera paint. "Tempera paint colors are very bright and bold," you tell your students. "Doesn't it seem that we should be bold, too, when we use them? Today we are going to use large brushes in order to make brave use of these wonderful colors!"

Use student ideas as energizers in awakening individual imaginations. "Wouldn't it be fun to use these bright, bold colors to paint pictures of bright, bold things? What could some of those things be?" As some children respond, others will begin to think, too. Replies will fly. A train! A tiger! Or a fall tree, a flower, a peacock, a robin red breast, even a silly hat!

Reach every individual as you explain the painting process. "We must cover our desks with newspaper and group together in fours with the people closest to us. We will each have a large brush, paper, and towels. We will share the paint in egg cartons! Point out that it is best to use light colors first, adding the darker colors next. Black and brown are best avoided until last of all. "As we switch from one color to another, we will wipe our brush clean on the paper towel. Water baths for brushes while painting can make the paint soupy. We want our paint to stay bold and bright!"

Appreciate each person as painting begins. One child passes out brushes, another towels, another paper, while two others cover the desks with newspapers. You spoon the paint into egg cartons and pass it out. You may discover that one student thinks he needs a thin brush. "Not today," you encourage him. "Thin brushes aren't bold!" Each painting is unique in idea or execution. Each student is happy when you compliment him.

Painting with large brushes is a success if students have bright ideas, the paintings are bold, and you are brave enough to attempt it. Using tempera with an entire class can require effort, but your organization and presentation make it a pleasure for everyone!

WHAT'S IMPORTANT TO ME
(emphasizing detail)

Materials needed: 12 × 18" manila paper, 3/4" easel brushes, 1/4" easel brushes, egg cartons, newspaper, red, yellow, blue, white, and black tempera, and towels. (See Figure 2-6.)

Figure 2-6
Detail

Pursuing Self-Expression through Painting

This activity provides practice in fine motor coordination, eye-hand coordination, translation, organization, and generalization.

Present the challenge by observing that an artist usually paints pictures of things that are special to him. "I'm sure that each of us can think of something that we like a lot which might not mean anything to anyone else."

Use student ideas as energizers, giving the children a chance to share ideas. "What is something that is important to you?" Answers will vary from a mini-bike to a particular place in the park; from an old stuffed animal to a dilapidated barn behind the house. Help your students not to be satisfied with stereotyped notions of beauty, such as a rose. Instead, encourage them to think of something with personal meaning. Develop with your class an awareness that there are many kinds of beauty.

Reach every individual as the class gets organized for painting. Desks are pushed into groups of four. Two children cover them with newspaper and others help pass out the large brushes, towels, and paper. Give each group an egg carton containing all colors but black. Green may also be included, or students can mix the color from blue and yellow in an empty section of the carton. "Clean your brushes on the towel while painting. Washing them adds too much water to the paint. When your paintings are nearly complete, I will give you each some black paint and a smaller brush to add the final details."

Appreciate each person now as energy and enthusiasm are directed to the painting process and the room becomes quiet. You may observe a child reverting to a cliché such as "triangle" houses and "lollipop" trees. He has drawn these many times and feels comfortable with them. Help him to grow artistically by encouraging him to talk before he begins to paint. "Your idea during the discussion was a good one! Nobody else thought of it. Why not try to paint it? Tell me how it looks." When most of the paintings are finished, distribute the black tempera and smaller brushes. "Let's pick out the most important parts of our pictures and outline them with the dark paint. Use just enough to emphasize the details."

Emphasizing detail is a success if the children's work shows attention to detail. Prepare a place for children to put their paintings to dry. Each child should drop his brush in the sink and toss away the towels and egg cartons wrapped in the newspaper. A couple of students can wash the brushes later. This avoids congestion at the sink. When the paintings are dry, have each child add a title and his name to one corner of the project. Then the pictures will be ready to display and enjoy.

PLEASED TO MEET YOU
(portraits)

Materials needed: 12 × 18" white drawing paper, 1/4" easel brushes, egg cartons, newspapers, towels, and red, yellow, blue, white, black, and brown tempera paints (fewer colors may be used). (See Figure 2-7.)

Figure 2-7
Portrait

Pursuing Self-Expression through Painting

This activity provides practice in fine motor coordination, eye-hand coordination, translation, organization, generalization, and integration.

Present the challenge by asking your students if they know what a portrait is. Explain that before the camera was invented, we depended upon artists to make pictures of people. Because of this we all can recognize George Washington and other people from history. Point out, however, that now cameras can take photos, so many artists try to describe an individual's **personality** in portraits, rather than just the way that individual looks. Perhaps you could find pictures of George Rouault's *The Old King*, Amadeo Modigliani's *Gypsy Woman with Baby*, Vincent Van Gogh's *Self-Portrait*, or Grant Wood's *American Gothic* in the library. Seeing these paintings will help your students to understand that there are many approaches to portrait paintings. Add another picture or two, such as Pablo Picasso's *Three Musicians*, and you will be giving them a mini-lesson in art appreciation as well as stimulating them to express individuality in painting.

Use student ideas as energizers by asking "How is your head shaped? Put one hand on your chin, another on the top of your head. Do both ends of your head feel the same? Right! You could say that we are 'egg heads'!" Have each child notice the special characteristics of the student across from him. Observe that a common mistake in drawing is placing the eyes too near the top of the head. They are really near the middle of the egg shape.

Reach every individual, providing him with directions and materials to tackle the problem. "Push your desks together face-to-face with the person closest to you. While you are painting his portrait, he will be painting yours!" Newspapers cover the desks, paints in egg cartons are shared, and brushes are wiped on towels when changing from one color to another. Explain that just head and shoulders portraits will be painted today.

Appreciate each person as painting begins. There may be a little silly behavior arising from embarrassment. Urge the students not to feel embarrassed about painting faces. Remind them that portraits need not look like photographs. Older children especially are inclined to be critical of their work. "Does a face really have an orange ring around it? No, it has the same color from one side to the other." Upper elementary students can mix this themselves by putting a dab of yellow and red in white paint. You may prefer to premix the flesh tone for younger children. Continue to help students be thoughtful. "Is your partner a happy person? Or is he often more serious and quiet? Can you show this in your painting?"

Portrait painting is a success if most children seem pleased with the results of their work. Have them title and sign their work—for example, *Tammy* by Susan. Cut the portraits out and display them on a bulletin board entitled, OUR CLASS.

Chapter 3

Tackling Techniques in Printmaking

LEAF PRINTS

Materials needed: 12 × 18" colored construction paper, paper towels, 3/4" easel brushes, egg cartons, tempera paints in several colors, and two or three leaves for each child. (See Figure 3-1.)

This activity provides practice in fine motor coordination, eye-hand coordination, auditory decoding, and sequencing.

Present the challenge by asking what it means to print. "Yes, printing does describe a way of writing, but it can also mean making more than one. A printing press is used to make many copies of a newspaper. There are many ways to print more than one of a picture, a design, or even this leaf!"

Use student ideas as energizers as the concept of printing is further explored. "Can you think of a way that we could print this leaf? Good! It can be placed under paper and rubbed with a crayon. Why does an impression of the leaf appear?" Do the experiment and show your students the result. They will

Basic Art Skills as Energizers

Figure 3-1
Leaf Print

quickly understand that this type of printing is possible because the veins of the leaf are raised. Explain that it is often necessary for part of a surface to be raised in order to print it. A typewriter works like that in striking through the ribbon onto the paper, and a fingerprint is made by the almost invisible lines in our fingers.

Reach every individual as you demonstrate the printing process to be used. "Today we are going to use paint to print our leaves. On which side of the leaf should we brush the paint?" The children will notice that the back of a leaf is the roughest part and, therefore, the best printing surface. "We will cover our desks with newspaper and push our printing paper to one side. We don't want it to get smudged. We can paint the

Tackling Techniques in Printmaking

leaves on the other side of our desks." Show students how to place the leaf face down on the newspaper, brush the back with paint, and transfer it to the printing paper with the painted side down. "Before I rub it, I am going to put a paper towel over the leaf so that I can keep my hands clean. Be sure that you use a clean towel, too, each time that you print a leaf!" Point out that the same leaf may be printed several times. Emphasize that using contrasting colors and overlapping the leaf prints will result in a pleasing arrangement.

Appreciate each person as the printmakers eagerly go to work. Desks have been grouped for sharing and several students pass paper, brushes, and towels. You give each group two or three colors of paint in half of an egg carton and then stand by to help if needed. You may find that a child has difficulty making a print and loses his patience. You show him how to apply the paint. "Too much is as bad as not enough. Be sure not to move the leaf while you rub. And be gentle!"

Leaf prints are a success if your students understand the concept of printmaking and add that word to their art vocabulary. The activity is especially appropriate in autumn when seasonal interest in falling leaves is an energizer. Leaf printing is a good introduction to printing, since the surface is already prepared. In other lessons in this chapter, students prepare their own printing surfaces.

POTATO PRINTS

Materials needed: potatoes, easel brushes, tempera paints in at least two colors, 12 × 18" paper on which to print (18 × 24" could be used with older students), nails, paper towels, and newspaper to cover the desks. (See Figure 3-2A.)

This activity provides practice in fine motor coordination, eye-hand coordination, auditory decoding, sequencing, translation, and generalization.

Present the challenge to your class by showing them a potato, a nail, and paint and explaining that these objects will be used to print a pattern. Their curiosity will be aroused!

Use student ideas as energizers in defining the important concept of this lesson. "When we speak of 'printing' in art class, what do we mean?" If your students have made the leaf prints in lesson 1 of this chapter, they will know the answer. "Yes,

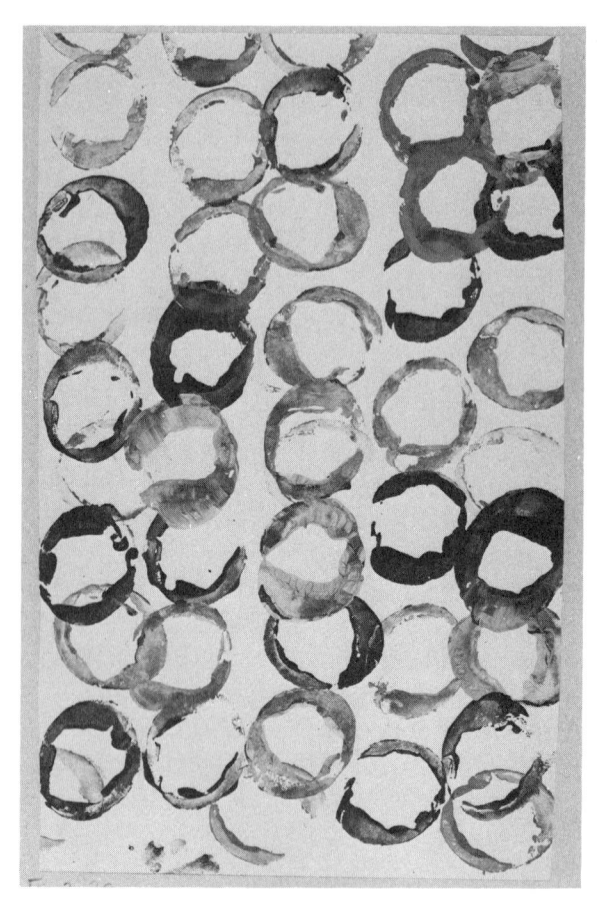

Figure 3-2A
Potato Print

printing is making more than one copy of a picture or design. This is easy to remember if we think of a printing press which is used to make hundreds of copies of a newspaper. Another example is a footprint that is an exact copy of a foot!"

Reach every individual by demonstrating how to print a potato. "In order to print, we need a flat surface on which the picture or design either stands out or is cut away," you begin. A potato sliced in two becomes the flat surface. A design is scraped into the surface with a nail. Scissors, wooden applicator sticks, or nail files all work fine, too. Knives can be used, but are not necessary. "Scrape away enough potato to make an interesting design. Be sure not to cut away too much, however. Some of the surface must stay smooth enough for us to paint and print." Remind students to try only

Tackling Techniques in Printmaking 49

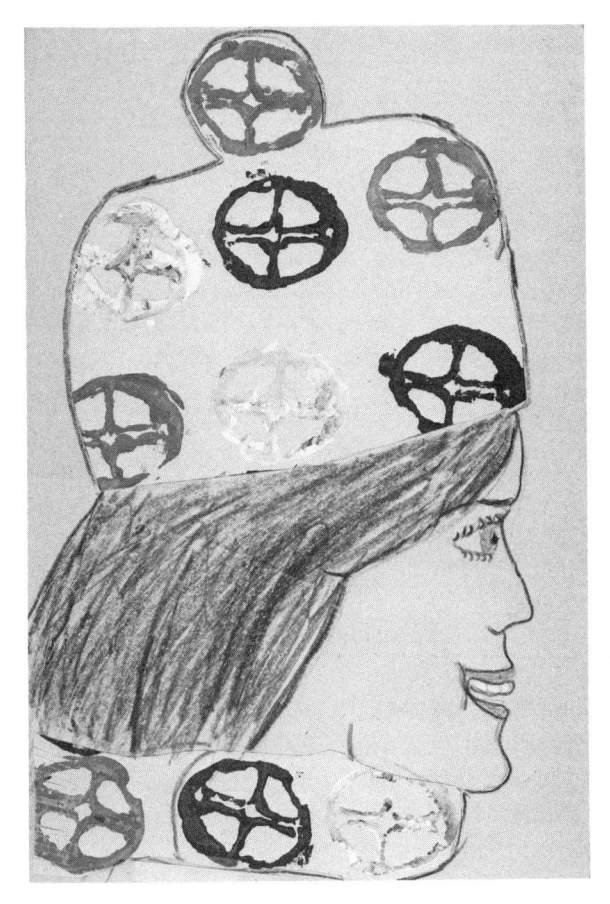

Figure 3-2B

designs. Attempting pictures with this process could be frustrating. When the design is done, press the potato on a towel to remove excess moisture, paint the surface, and print it several times on the paper. When the image becomes faint, paint the potato again. Have each student take half a potato, a nail, a brush, towels, and paper for printing as he returns to his newspaper covered desk. You can pass out the paint.

Appreciate each person as the printers work out their designs and begin to print. Admire their efforts. "Using both colors of paint on the potato makes an interesting print," you tell one. "Alternating colors is effective, too." Show these examples to the class. Successful student work can be a good energizer. "One color is attractive also. Just decide which you would rather do and continue until your paper is filled."

Figure 3-2C

Potato printing is a success if your students understand the concept of repeated printing and their colorful papers prove it! These prints could be used for bookcovers or wrapping paper. Another day each child could use his pattern as part of a picture by cutting out curtains, clothes, or wallpaper and adding scrap paper details. (See Figures 3-2B and 3-2C.)

SEASONAL STYROFOAM PRINTS

Materials needed: pencils or nails, styrofoam meat or produce trays, 8 × 12" colored construction paper for printing, paint, brushes, towels, and newspaper to cover the desks. (See Figure 3-3.) In this activity as well as the three which follow, brayers, inking trays, and printing ink could be used with good results. These materials are designed for printing and are easy to control. They are not always available, however, so printing methods in which paint can be substituted have been suggested. Impressions of the printing surfaces in these lessons may also be made by rubbing with the side of a crayon.

This activity provides practice in fine motor coordination, eye-hand coordination, auditory decoding, sequencing, association, translation, organization, and generalization.

Tackling Techniques in Printmaking

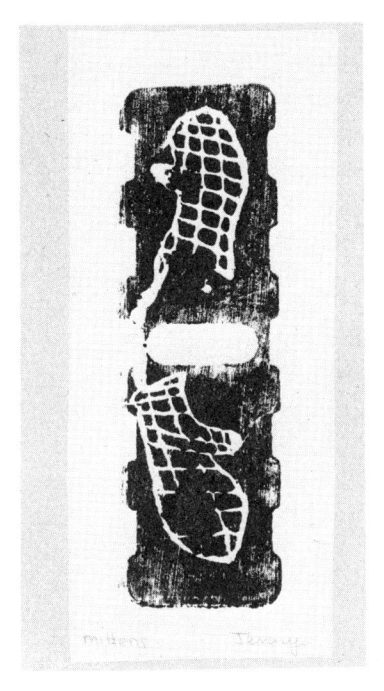

Figure 3-3
Styrofoam Print

Present the challenge to your students of learning more about printing. "When we speak of printing in art, we mean making more than one of a particular picture or design," you explain. "In order to make many, we usually begin with a flat surface in which the design or picture is either cut away or raised. A simple example of printing is putting a coin or a leaf under paper and rubbing over it with a crayon. One can also cut a picture into a styrofoam tray with a pencil point or a nail and use that for a printing surface. Want to give it a try?"

Use student ideas as energizers in selecting subjects for the pictures to be printed. "Each season of the year is special. What are some things which we associate with this season?" This type of discussion now will avoid the "I-don't-know-what-to-make" syndrome later. Show the students how to make a drawing on the outside of the bottom of the styrofoam tray, cutting in with the pencil point or a nail. "Be sure not to cut through the tray completely," you warn. If a trademark is embossed on the bottom of the tray, it can be disguised by drawing over it and using it as part of the picture. "Let's keep our drawings simple," you suggest. "Including too much could make our print confusing." When the drawing is done, the printing surface is ready.

Reach every individual with a thoughtful demonstration—the best energizer. "We will all cover our desks with newspaper. We should have a container of paint, a brush, several sheets of colored construction paper on which to print, and of course our styrofoam surface." Emphasize that the desk top should be organized to avoid a mess. "Let's put the tray, brush, and paint on one side of our desks. Keep the other side clear and clean for printing. The paper can be put on the chair, since it is easier to stand while printing." Show the students how to brush a coat of paint over the picture and out to the edge of the tray. The tray is then moved to the clean side of the desk. Quickly, before the paint begins to dry, colored construction paper is placed over the paint and rubbed gently but firmly—also out to the edges. As the paper is peeled off, the print appears! "We cannot stack our prints up until they are dry," you point out. "Why not put them under your desk and chair until you finish printing. Be careful not to step on them!" This will avoid excess movement in the room.

Appreciate every person by helping individuals with technical problems. One may be using too much paint, another not enough. You may observe that one needs to cut further into the tray, and still another may require more patience in rubbing the paper. When a student achieves several successful prints, have him wrap his tray in the newspaper over his desk and dispose of it. Brushes and paint can be placed in the sink for a clean-up crew and the prints moved to a designated area of the room to dry.

Styrofoam prints are a success if the children are pleased with their efforts. The room should be clean and orderly, so that the only evidence of earlier activity is in the many colorful pictures left to dry. Have the students sign them at the bottom in pencil, as artists do their prints. A title comes first, followed by the date and the signature. The back of the prints could be used for note paper or as invitations for a special program. The prints could also be covers for papers taken home.

CHRISTMAS CARDS PRINTED FROM OAK TAG AND STRING

Materials needed: 4 × 6" oak tag, string, white glue, brushes, tempera paint, 8 × 12" colored construction paper on which to

Tackling Techniques in Printmaking 53

Figure 3-4
String and Oak Tag

print, towels, and newspaper to cover the desks. (See Figure 3-4.)

This activity provides practice in fine motor coordination, eye-hand coordination, auditory decoding, sequencing, association, translation, and generalization.

Present the challenge to your students by asking if they would like to send a Christmas card to each of their friends and relatives. Point out that making all those cards would take a long time. Explain that commercial cards, or ones purchased at a store, are printed by machine. "We have no printing machine to make many copies of a card," you continue. "Besides, handmade cards are very special. We could use string, glue, and oak tag to make a picture or design and print it by hand. Want to find out how?"

Use student ideas as energizers after you explain the process. "We usually need a flat surface with the picture or design either cut away or raised in order to print. This half sheet of oak tag is a good size for a card. We will use this for our flat surface. We can use string and glue to make a raised picture or design. What are some symbols of Christmas?" Evergreen trees, ornaments, bells, candles, and stockings come to mind immediately. Holiday enthusiasm is always a good energizer!

Reach every individual with a demonstration. "I'll make a candle," you begin. "I will sketch it lightly with pencil on the oak tag. I won't use much detail, but will pay attention to the shape. I can't use words because they come out backwards in the print and can't be read." When the sketch is complete, glue is squeezed over the lines of the drawing. The string is then placed on the glue. If there are not enough dispenser bottles of glue for the class to share, the glue may be poured on pieces of scrap paper and applied in lines with applicator or Popsicle sticks. "We must wait until the glue is dry before printing," you caution your students. "You can make your pictures or designs today and print them tomorrow."

Appreciate each person as the string and oak tag surfaces are prepared. Help the children to think of as many holiday motifs as possible. Remind students that parts of the picture will print only if the surface is raised. Check each child's work to be sure that it will print well. The third lesson in this chapter, "Seasonal Styrofoam Prints," contains complete directions for organizing, accomplishing, and cleaning up after the printing process.

Oak tag and string printed cards are a success if each child makes several good prints. It works well to print the cards on 8 × 12" sheets of construction paper in colors which contrast with the paint. This results in a wide margin around the picture. A greeting may be written at the bottom. If the paper is then folded 1/3 of the way down from the top and 1/3 of the way up from the bottom, it becomes its own envelope. This process can be used to make cards for any special occasion.

OAK TAG PRINTS

Materials needed: 8 × 12" oak tag, white glue, scissors, paper on which to print, tempera paint, easel brushes, and newspaper to cover the desks. (See Figure 3-5.)

This activity provides practice in fine motor coordination, eye-hand coordination, auditory decoding, sequencing, and generalization.

Present the challenge to your students of combining oak tag, glue, paint, and paper to produce a print. "We know that there are many kinds of prints," you begin. "What are some of them? Sure, fingerprints and footprints are good examples! In art, prints are copies of a picture or design in the same way that your footprint is a copy of your foot! We need a special surface

Tackling Techniques in Printmaking

Figure 3-5
Teddy Bear

from which to make the print, however. We are going to make ours from this oak tag and glue."

Use student ideas as energizers as you help the class consider what characteristics the printing surface must have. "Why is it that our hands leave fingerprints when we touch something? Yes, each of us has a pattern of tiny raised lines on his fingers unlike those belonging to anyone else! We could say then, that having part of the surface raised makes printing possible."

Reach every individual as you explain how to transform the oak tag into an appropriate printing surface. "We can cut the oak tag in two pieces. One piece will be the printing surface. The parts of the picture or design will be cut from the other piece. These will be glued to the first piece to create the raised printing surface."

Appreciate each person as you provide them with directions, materials, and subject matter for the project. "We will be printing many copies of the picture which we make. It might be fun to make a picture of something that we wish we had a lot of. I'll make mine of a kitten. What will you choose?" Show students how to cut the basic shape and necessary details from one half of the oak tag, then glue them on the other. Your demonstration will serve as an energizer if you keep the design as simple as possible. Too many small parts are distracting. Remind children that only the raised parts of the picture will print. Once everyone understands the procedure, pass out the oak tag, scissors, and glue. Printing is best saved for the next day when the glue is completely dry. The printing process is identical to that described in the third lesson of this chapter, "Seasonal Styrofoam Prints." As suggested, 8 × 12" colored construction paper works well.

Oak tag relief prints are a success if your explanation, demonstration, and organization bring each individual through the project with pleasure. The room should be clean—the prints proudly displayed. Now the pleasure is yours!

STENCIL SILHOUETTE PRINTS

Materials needed: 8 × 12" oak tag, 8 × 12" paper on which to print, tempera paint, wide easel brushes, towels, and newspaper to cover the desks. If stencil knives are available, they could be used with older groups, but place cardboard under the oak tag while cutting. (See Figure 3-6.)

This activity provides practice in fine motor coordination, eye-hand coordination, auditory decoding, sequencing, translation, and generalization.

Figure 3-6
Just Plain Plump

Tackling Techniques in Printmaking

Present the challenge of tackling another printing technique to your students. You can begin by saying, "We have learned that printing means making more than one copy of a particular picture or design. We discovered that in most cases printing must be done from a flat surface on which the picture or design has been raised or cut away." If your students have made prints before, review this information with them. If this is their first experience with printing, be sure that they understand what it is about. A basic explanation is found in the first lesson of this chapter.

Use student ideas as energizers as you explain that a stencil is a piece of oak tag or cardboard with letters, a design, or a picture cut from it. Color in the form of crayons, paint, or ink is pushed through the cut-out portion and printed onto the paper beneath. Point out that in stencil printing the shape of the design is most important. "Since we are primarily concerned with shape in making stencil prints, let's think of some objects which have unusual or distinctive silhouettes.

Reach every individual as students speak up. Be sure that a wide range of possibilities has been considered—from trees to tortoises to two-wheel bikes. Each person must have an idea of his own. "We will draw the object on the oak tag. Your drawing should be large enough to include details of the shape. Next we cut it out. Don't cut through the edge of the paper! Poke the scissor point right through the middle. The remaining oak tag frame becomes our stencil." Show the children how to place it on the printing paper and brush the paint through the stencil onto the paper underneath. "Be careful not to use too much paint or it will leak around the stencil. The paint must be brushed away from the inside edge of the stencil toward the center of the paper under it. And remember to always use the stencil with the same side up! If you turn it over after you have started, you will get paint on your paper!"

Appreciate each person by watching the students as they work to see if they all have an appropriate idea. Some subjects cannot be adapted to a stencil. It is generally best to prepare the stencils on one day and print them on the next. Too many processes could be complicated and confusing. A suggested printing procedure is given in lesson 3, "Seasonal Styrofoam Prints." Using it after a recess would give you a chance to get the room set up. You might advise younger students to use crayons to print their stencils. Admittedly, paint can be hard

to control. You are the best judge of your students' abilities.
Stencil prints are a success if your students follow directions and complete the process. There is much to be gained beyond the picture-product from such art activity. Intangibles like the ability to follow directions, solve problems, and concentrate are taught. Moreover, in an age of instant breakfast and instant T.V. entertainment, the children learn patience. We must avoid thinking of art as a "paint, paper, presto! picture situation." Through more complex precedures, an appreciation of skill and craftsmanship can be acquired.

TISSUE PAPER PRINTS

Materials needed: 12 × 18" colored construction paper, white drawing paper cut to about 6 × 9", assorted tissue paper scraps in bright colors, easel brushes, water, and water containers. (See Figure 3-7.)

This activity provides practice in fine motor coordination, eye-hand coordination, auditory decoding, translation, organization, sequencing, and generalization.

Present the challenge to your students of using a simple method to make a colorful copy of a print. "Printing means making more

Figure 3-7
Tissue Prints

Tackling Techniques in Printmaking

than one of a picture or design. There are many ways to print. All of them require a specially prepared surface like a stencil or a linoleum block, color of some kind like paint or ink, and pressure," you explain. "Today white drawing paper will be our color and the pressure will come from rubbing."

Use student ideas as energizers while you discuss what things would be fun to include in the prints. "Let's make our topic 'Things That Float or Fly,'" you suggest. An imaginative but specific topic will help each child to select a subject more readily than a whole range of unrelated ideas. "What could some of these be?" The energetic response may include fish, seaweed, pond lillies, boats, bugs, bats, balloons, and birds!

Reach every individual by demonstrating the printing process. Unlike many other methods, tissue paper prints can be done in one session. "We will each have two pieces of white drawing paper, several large tissue paper scraps in bright colors, scissors, a brush, and water. We will cut the parts of the picture that we wish to make from the tissue paper. The cut tissue paper picture is then carefully arranged on one of the pieces of drawing paper. Next we brush water over each part of our picture. While it is still wet, put the other piece of drawing paper on top of it. Now rub!" When the paper on top is lifted off, a colorful impression of the tissue paper beneath remains. The wet tissue is peeled away from the paper underneath. Exposed is another print, identical to the first. The pressure of rubbing has caused the color to spread, changing the shape of the original cut paper picture. "It looks as if it might be under water or among clouds high in the sky, doesn't it?"

Appreciate each person as all follow your directions. The materials are ready so everyone can take what he needs as he returns to his seat. Students will eagerly start to cut the tissue paper pictures as you pass out the water. Encourage the children to avoid detail, concentrating instead on color and shape. As the prints are completed, you will find that some students wish to use crayons or marker to add details to the prints. Although a professional artist would not do it, retouching a print can help certain elementary students to better express their ideas.

Tissue paper prints are a success if colors have been blended to create new colors, and shapes have been changed to different shapes. Each printmaker can mount his products together on a sheet of 12 × 18″ colored construction paper. A title and signature are then added. Display the prints in your classroom. Observing and discussing them are a pleasant end to this project.

Chapter 4

Solving Problems in Sculpture

SCRAPWOOD ANIMALS

Materials needed: assorted small wood scraps (available at wood product factories, mills, or brought from home), white glue, nails, buttons, bits of yarn and cloth, paint, and markers for finishing details. (See Figure 4-1.)

This activity provides practice in eye-hand coordination, organization, translation, and generalization.

Present the challenge to your children of creating a curious classroom zoo from scraps of wood. "We have several boxes of small pieces of wood as well as other leftovers like yarn, buttons, and cloth to work with. Let's use our imaginations in combining these materials. How many different animals do you think that we can make?"

Use student ideas as energizers while you select a few scraps and see what they suggest. "Does this yellow yarn remind you of something? Yes! I thought of a lion's mane too! Which piece of wood should we use for a head? Sure, we could have a square one, although a lion's head isn't really square—it is large and heavy looking. A block will give that effect."

Figure 4-1
Scrapwood Animal

Reach every individual by encouraging all to offer suggestions as you sort through more scraps. "You say that cloth triangles will make good ears? I'll glue them on and we'll see how they look. What could we use for the back? Yes, I believe that long piece of wood will work very well. A yarn-braid tail? Good idea! Let's try it." As you talk, the lion takes shape. "What about some legs? Sure, we can glue on these long thin scraps so that our creature can stand up," you continue. "How could we make him appear to be lying down? Right, shorter pieces glued beside the body would do. Or we could draw the legs with a marker."

Appreciate each person as he decides which animal to make and takes turns selecting a few scraps to get started with. Each student can return for more if necessary. Dispenser bottles of glue can be shared or the glue may be poured onto scraps of paper and passed out. "There are many kinds of animals in a zoo. Our zoo will be a good one because almost every one of you has a different idea." Circulate among the students offering assistance where needed and plenty of praise. Encouragement is a fine energizer.

Solving Problems in Sculpture

Scrapwood animals are a success if students take pleasure in the creatures. Constructing a three-dimensional object is always fun, especially for elementary students. It is a challenging and novel experience, yet well within each individual's ability. Why not display the creatures along your window sills? Enjoy the zoo parade!

PAPIER-MÂCHÉ CHARACTER HEADS

Materials needed: wheat (wallpaper) paste, 6 or 8 large tin cans from the hot lunch program, plastic beach pails or other big containers, water, masking tape, and plenty of newspapers. Tempera paints, egg cartons, brushes, yarn, and cloth scraps will be used to complete the project. (See Figure 4-2A.)

This activity provides practice in auditory decoding, translation, and generalization.

Present the challenge of making a three-dimensional portrait to your students. Explain that a dimension is an edge which can be measured. "For example, this paper is tall and wide," you say, holding a piece up for inspection. "That means that it has two dimensions—height and width. If I turn it sideways, you can hardly see it and you surely couldn't measure it!" Point out that painting and drawing are two-dimensional while sculpture has depth, the third dimension. "The portraits we make will be three-dimensional paper and paste sculptures!"

Figure 4-2A
Papier-Mâché Character Heads

Use student ideas as energizers in deciding which characters might be portrait possibilities. Listen to each suggestion, helping individuals to select a subject with distinctive features. "Good! Mickey Mouse or Donald Duck would be great. The big ears and large bill make both easy to recognize!" A student asks if he can "make up" a character. "That would be fun too," you answer.

Reach every individual by explaining that papier-mâché is wet and limp, so it must be put over a base, one layer at a time. When one layer is dry, another is added. When the sculpture is complete, it will be nearly as hard as wood. Demonstrate how to make a base by crumpling a sheet of newspaper into a ball and wrapping it with masking tape or string to hold the shape. Give each child paper and tape or string. When everyone has a base prepared, group the desks in fours or sixes, cover them with newspaper and provide a container of wheat paste and a supply of strips at each station. Show the students the way to dip newspaper strips in the paste and apply them one at a time until the base is covered. Have a newspaper-covered area in the room ready for children to put their sculptures to dry. Suggest that everyone write his name on a scrap of paper and stick it on his work. Collect the paste cans and wrap the newspaper from the desks around the remaining strips to toss away.

Appreciate each person as the project progresses. When the first layer of papier-mâché is dry, regroup for another session. Now is the time to add important details. Newspaper dampened with paste and squeezed into a ball becomes a round nose—stretch it out and you have a long nose! Fold it into two half-circles and place them on the side of the head for "people" ears. Fold it in triangles, put them on top, and you have "cat" ears. A twisted scrap of papier-mâché arched on the forehead is an eyebrow. Turn it into an "O" for a surprised mouth or make a wide, happy grin. The wet paper can be modeled almost as easily as clay. (See Figure 4-2B.) It is extremely important to secure each detail by smoothing a piece of papier-mâché over it. If the sculpture seems too wet, add some dry paper. Stiffness for parts like long or large ears can be achieved by using dry paper shapes with a layer or two of pasted paper over them. Careful smoothing of the sculpture as one works will provide a good surface for painting. When the second layer is dry, most students will be ready to com-

Solving Problems in Sculpture 65

Figure 4-2B
Papier-Mâché Puppet Heads

plete the project with paint, paste, cloth, and yarn for hair.
Papier-mâché character heads are a success if each one portrays a particular personality. Each head should be mounted on a scrapwood base. The children will have fun naming their creations and writing a few sentences about them on squares of paper. These can be glued to every base. What an amusing and colorful assemblage! You always knew that there were some real "characters" in your room, didn't you?

PAPIER-MÂCHÉ BOTTLE PEOPLE

Materials needed: wheat (wallpaper) paste, large containers such as cans from the hot lunch program or plastic beach pails, an empty bottle for each child, masking tape, and plenty of newspaper. Paints, brushes, yarn, and assorted paper scraps are used for completing the project. (See Figure 4-3A.)

This activity provides practice in auditory decoding, translation, and generalization.

Present the challenge to your students of turning a bottle into a storybook person. Have the necessary materials ready for a demonstration—always an effective energizer. "By adding wheat paste and newspaper to bottles, we can create all kinds of characters. Want to see how it is done?"

Figure 4-3A
Papier-Mâché Bottle People

Use student ideas as energizers as you show your class how to begin the project. "What would we need to add first in order to make this shape look more like a person?" Hold the bottle up. "Yes, we do need a head!" Tear a sheet of newspaper in two. Crumple one half into a ball and hold it at the top of the neck of the bottle. "I'm going to use the other half to secure the head to the body," you explain. Place the paper over the top of the newspaper "head" and smooth it down over the sides of the bottle. "At this point, it helps to work in pairs. Will you be my partner?" Have a student hold the paper around the neck of the bottle. "The neck of the bottle will be a good neck for our character," you point out. Use three strips of masking tape to attach the newspaper to the bottle base. One strip goes around the neck and one around the waist. The third strip is stretched from one side of the bottle under the bottom and up the other side. "This will be the base for our paste and newspaper people. Do you each have an idea of what character you would like to make?" (See Figure 4-3B.)

Reach every individual as you help your students prepare bases for their sculptures. Give each a sheet of newspaper and stick

Solving Problems in Sculpture 67

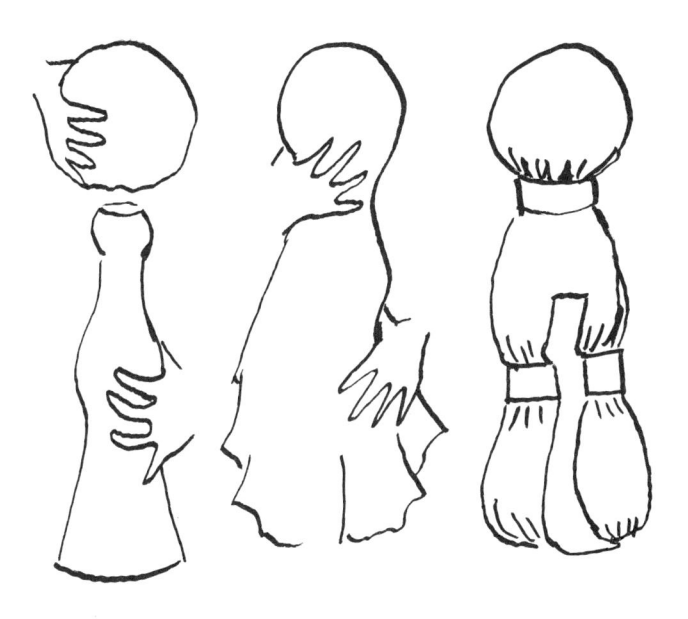

Figure 4-3B
Bottle People

three strips of masking tape to the side of every desk where it will be ready when needed. Remind them that this first step is best done in pairs. "Be careful to keep the bottles on the desk," you warn. "They will break if you let them slip." When all the bases are ready, have the children push their desks into groups of four or six and cover them with newspaper. Show students how to dip hand-sized pieces of torn newspaper into the paste, scraping any excess on the edge of the container. It should be wet, but not soggy. The pieces are then smoothed onto the base until it is entirely covered with papier-mâché. Put a container of paste and a pile of torn newspaper pieces in the center of each group. The children are anxious to go to work!

Appreciate each person, each "bottle person" that is! Once the first layer is dry, it is time to use more papier-mâché to add the distinctive details. Now the individual characteristics of the creatures will emerge. Organize the room for working. Show the students how to put new parts on their people. Some suggestions for making facial details are given in the second lesson of this chapter, "Character Heads." Arms may be made by rolling dry newspaper scraps into the desired length, then attaching them to the body with more newspaper that has been dipped in the wheat paste. A clown hat can be made by rolling a piece of dry newspaper into a cone and covering it with paste-wet paper. Ask the students to think of ways to make other types of hats and encourage the children to be problem solvers. "Be sure that your sculpture has a smooth surface and that all parts are securely attached before you put it to dry," you warn. It is a good idea to check this for young children by handling their work.

Bottle people are a success if "people" distinctly different from one another appear as paint is added. You should caution your class to keep the paint jobs simple in order to avoid a cluttered looking product. Yarn, buttons, and cloth provide the finishing touches. Now each bottle creature reveals two personalities—his and his sculptor's!

LIGHT BULB BIRDS

Materials needed: wheat (wallpaper) paste, large containers such as cans from the hot lunch program or plastic beach pails, newspaper, and an old light bulb for each student. Paints and brushes are needed to complete the project. (See Figure 4-4A.)

Figure 4-4A
Light Bulb Birds

Solving Problems in Sculpture 69

This activity provides practice in auditory decoding, translation, and generalization.

Present the challenge to your students of using a burned out light bulb as a base for papier-mâché birds. "Papier-mâché is just pieces of newspaper which have been dipped in wallpaper paste," you begin. "By itself it is limp and mushy. That's why we must always shape it over a base. This base is called an **armature**," you add. "An armature works like the skeleton in your bodies. It is an inside framework which serves as a support."

Use student ideas as energizers as you discuss with your class the way in which the light bulbs can be transformed into armatures. "Can you see any similarities between the shape of this light bulb and that of a bird? Sure. The large round part could be the breast. How could we make it look more like a bird? Yes, a head and a tail would do the trick!"

Reach every individual by demonstrating how to prepare a base from the bulb. Crumple a piece of newspaper into a ball the right size for a bird's head. Attach this to the bulb—or body—at the side of the roundest part. Wrap the sheet of newspaper over the head and around the body. One strip of masking tape goes around the "neck" of the bird. Smooth the paper over the bulb. Another piece of tape goes around the neck of the light bulb. The remaining tuft of paper looks like a tail. Finally, give each child a sheet of newspaper and two strips of tape.

Appreciate each person as the project progresses. Student's desks are grouped and covered with newspapers. A large container of wheat paste and a pile of newspaper scraps is at the center of each station. Show them how to prepare the paste and dip the newspaper in it. Explain that each piece of paper added must have all lumps and wrinkles rubbed away. The surface must be smooth enough to paint when the sculpture is hard and dry. Roll up your sleeves and demonstrate how three or four hand-sized pieces of paste-wet newspaper can be applied over the base and quickly complete the first layer of papier-mâché. (See Figure 4-4B.) Big or little, skinny or fat triangles are all that are needed now. Fold them out of dry newspaper, cover, and attach them with more newspaper moistened in paste for wings, tail feathers, a beak, and even a comb! You will discover that some students may need help with shaping and attaching parts, so don't dry your hand yet! Check each bird as it is put to dry, being sure that wings and beaks are securely attached and the surface is smooth enough to paint.

Figure 4-4B
Light Bulb Bird

Light bulb birds are a success if your students now understand how to work with an armature using papier-mâché. When the birds have dried and been brightly painted, decide whether to glue them to scrapwood bases or hang them, mobile style, from a tree branch. Weren't those bulb birds a bright idea?

FOIL AND CARDBOARD RELIEFS

Materials needed: 8 × 12" sheets of oak tag, scraps of corrugated cardboard boxes and other cardboard, scissors, white glue, and aluminum foil. (See Figure 4-5.)

This activity provides practice in fine motor coordination, eye-hand coordination, translation, organization, and generalization.

Present the challenge to your class of making a circle sculpture that really isn't round. "That sounds confusing, doesn't it? But some sculptures are quite flat and are intended to decorate a wall," you point out. "We call this type of sculpture a relief." Add that a relief is considered sculpture because its surface is not smooth. Some parts are recessed and others protrude, providing the three dimensions of height, width, and depth. "Today we are going to use cardboard and aluminum foil to construct relief sculpture," you explain. "The subject of the sculpture will be something that has a circle."

Use student ideas as energizers and start the ball rolling by asking, "What are some things that are round?" A wheel, an orange, a pumpkin, or a plump face are all good examples! A relief

Solving Problems in Sculpture

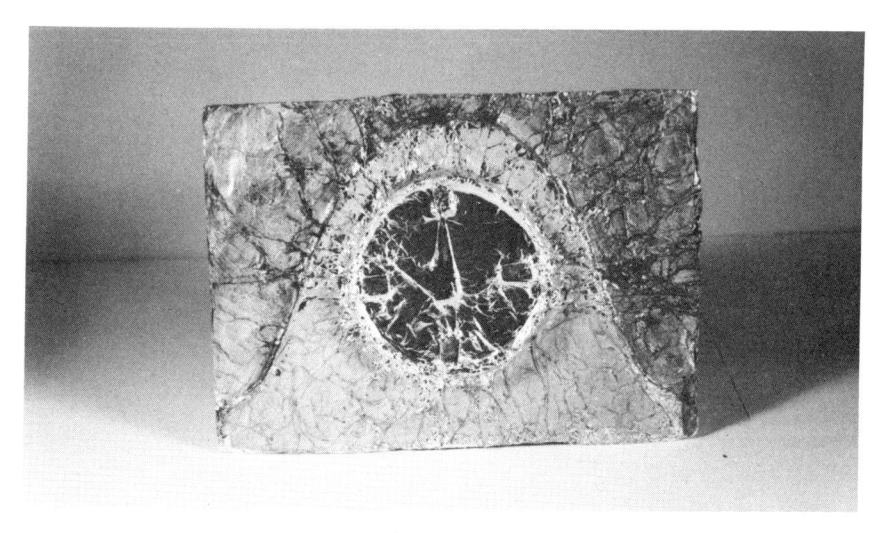

Figure 4-5
Foil Relief Sculpture

sculpture of an orange alone wouldn't be very interesting, would it? "How could we improve our design?" you continue. "Right, we could show the orange as part of a tree, in a fruit bowl, or in somebody's hand! We must be sure that our sculptures tell how the circle is being used."

Reach every individual by showing the children how to make their sculptures. The 8 × 12" oak tag is the background. "I'm going to use my circle as part of a car," you begin, cutting one from cardboard. "There! I have a wheel. Now I need to cut out the rest. I want another wheel and the body of the car to begin with. Next I can add more details such as hubcaps and door handles." Point out that the top layer of paper can be peeled from the corrugated cardboard, providing another texture. Small strips, dots, or squares of cardboard can also give a textured effect. Show students how several identical shapes can be cut using the first one as a pattern. They are then glued one on top of the other. "These will stick out farther from the surface. Some of the cut out parts should be quite flat, others thick," you observe. When all the parts are glued in place, put a sheet of aluminum foil over the relief, folding it around the edges. Rub the foil gently until it conforms to all the contours of the cut cardboard underneath.

Appreciate each person after materials are distributed and everyone is busy constructing with cardboard. Encourage each child to employ a variety of textures, as well as thick and thin parts, in his arrangement. You will find something special about each relief, and should tell the students. Your interest is a great energizer.

Foil and cardboard reliefs are a success if young children manage the materials and express an idea. Pieces of 8 × 12" construction paper can be glued to the back, concealing rough folded foil edges and giving the product a finished appearance. Make damp towels and trays of water paints available to the class. Some students may decide to dip a towel-covered finger in the paint and rub color on some parts of their relief. Stand the sculptures along your window sill or staple them to your bulletin board. It's fun to have the sculptures about circles all around!

CARDBOARD CARTON CREATURES

Materials needed: a large cardboard carton for each child, colored construction paper, paper, cloth and yarn scraps, white glue, scissors, tempera paints, and brushes. Empty paper towel tubes come in handy, too. (See Figure 4-6.)

This activity provides practice in fine motor coordination, eye-

Figure 4-6
Huge Cardboard Carton Creatures

Solving Problems in Sculpture 73

hand coordination, translation, organization, generalization, and integration.

Present the challenge to your children of constructing dramatically large creatures from cartons. The novelty of working in three dimensions is always an energizer for elementary students. Cartons are usually discarded and are available for the asking at supermarkets. Ask each child to bring one in. The request alone is enough to excite a child's curiousity!

Use student ideas as energizers by taking a look at some of the boxes to see what they suggest. "What about this long, low box? An alligator? Good thinking! What does this square box bring to mind? Yes, it would be fun to make an elephant from it. Sure, that tall, narrow box could become a zoo-keeper. With all these animals, we will need one!"

Reach every individual by suggesting various ways to begin the project. This is an activity which older elementary students can manage very well by themselves and find extremely rewarding. Younger children may require more individual assistance from their teacher. You might prefer to have them work in groups of two or three on one animal. "First we will need to cut away some of the box to make legs," you point out. Cut a half circle in each of the four sides of the box. The creature will stand on the remaining four corners. Blunt school scissors will not do the trick. Let older children share teacher's shears or a mat knife. Help younger ones with this. "Next we may need a neck. Some animals have long ones! Here are some paper tubes to be attached with tape, or you can roll a sheet of construction paper into a long, thin tube. If your creature has a short neck, why not omit it and attach the head right to the box," you suggest. Show students how to roll construction paper into cone or cylinder shapes for heads. Cones are good for animals with pointed noses like foxes or giraffes. Cylinders make good hippo heads, for example. Once the head and body have been constructed, only the details remain to be done. That's child's play!

Appreciate each person as you help with finishing touches. Paper triangles or circles pasted in place make good ears. Be sure that eye color contrasts with the color of the animal. Bright eyes add a lot of personality and expression! Braided yarn tails are fun to make. Fat sides or humped backs may be fashioned by cutting large circles from construction paper.

Cut several darts around the edge. Glue or staple them over newspaper stuffing to the top or sides of the box. Now you can pass out the brushes and paint, or you may prefer to have the children do the painting later, a few at a time.

Cardboard carton creatures are a success if the children show they love expressing ideas in a big way. The large sculptures fill your room, transforming it into a zoo. Enjoy it for a day or two, then share it with the rest of the school. Display the creatures in the hall, library, or cafeteria.

FOIL FIGURES

Materials needed: aluminum foil, scissors, and cardboard cut into geometric shapes about 2" wide. (See Figure 4-7A.)

This activity provides practice in auditory discrimination, generalization, and translation.

Figure 4-7A
Foil Figures

Present the challenge by showing your class a photo or drawing of a person or persons in action. Try to select one that is dramatic and will capture their interest. Ask them to tell you how they know the person pictured is moving. Some child will

Solving Problems in Sculpture

notice that the knees and arms are bent. "Right! That's how we are able to move—by bending our bodies!"

Use student ideas as energizers and ask if they could go upstairs without bending their knees. Let one student try to climb on his chair with stiff legs. "How could we sit if we couldn't bend from the hips?" One in every class will insist that he can. Let him demonstrate and everyone will see how impractical it is. "How could you eat your cereal if you couldn't bend your arm? You'd have to put your nose in the bowl like a dog!"

Reach every individual by demonstrating how to use aluminum foil to create a "mini" sculpture of a person in action. A square of foil is cut in three places; one cut 1/3 of the way up from the center of the bottom and two cuts 1/3 of the way down from the top. The foil is then gently crumpled from the sides. The cut at the bottom becomes two legs; the three parts at the top become two arms and the head. Show students how to be gentle, or the foil may become a wad. Next, the arms and legs are pressed and modeled to the desired size, and the head shaped into a ball. (See Figure 4-7B.) The completed figure can be bent at the elbows, knees, and hips to show action. These action figures may be attached with white glue to a cardboard base. Drawing a diagram on the board might help some individuals.

Figure 4-7B
Foil Figures

Appreciate each person as you pass out the foil and ask what action he is going to show. Energize the class by having students with unusual ideas share them. You may discover that some children have difficulty crumpling the foil. Repeat step by step directions, watching and encouraging them while they do it themselves. Help each student complete his work by showing how to make a skirt for a majorette or a cape for batman, for example. A scrap of foil twisted onto the figure does the trick. Once the figures are secure on the base, suggest that students name their mini-sculptures, writing the title and their own names on the cardboard.

Foil figures are a success if the children understand the concept of showing action by bending the joints of the body. This activity could also complement a gesture drawing lesson—Part I, Chapter 1.

TOTEM POLES

Materials needed: tempera paints, brushes, towels, water, newspaper, glue, empty oatmeal containers, and nearly square cardboard cartons. Photos of totem poles and other American Indian art would be helpful, too. (See Figure 4-8.)

Figure 4-8
Totem Poles

Solving Problems in Sculpture

This activity provides practice in fine motor coordination, eye-hand coordination, auditory decoding, association, translation, organization, generalization, and integration.

Present the challenge to your students of turning old cartons into individual interpretations of totem poles. Explain that the American Indians carved these tall, handsome sculptures from trees and then painted them. Totem poles were important as part of the Indian's religion. They honored the powerful spirits which Indians believed belong to each animal. The Indians hoped that the spirits would be pleased with their art and continue to send them game to hunt for their food, clothing, and shelter.

Use student ideas as energizers as you discuss how totem poles can be made from objects found right in your classroom. Have each child bring in an old box from home. Boxes about a foot square are best, but smaller or larger cartons will do (cylindrical oatmeal or cornmeal cartons are ideal). "The figures on totem poles represented animals that Indians hunted and admired. What would some of these be?" you ask. "Yes, the deer and buffalo were hunted for meat and fur. Fish were another source of food. And eagles and hawks were admired for their speed and grace in flight. These surely should be included in our totem poles!"

Reach every individual by giving each one directions and materials needed to make his part of this project. "Everyone has a box that will be one section of a totem pole. Like the figures in Indian art, it should represent a spirit. Characteristics of men and animals alike may be combined in these creatures," you point out. If possible, show the students pictures of totem poles from an encyclopedia or other source. Note how the figures have been stylized to fit the contour of the tree from which the pole was carved. "We will have to do the same thing," you explain, "to make our creature conform to the shape of our box!" Group the desks for sharing, cover them with newspaper, and pass out the paints and brushes.

Appreciate each person as the parts of the poles are painted. You may need to remind some students that a simple paint job is usually most effective. Each box should be painted entirely in one or two colors only, using a large brush. As the box dries, details may be painted on with other colors. Help students to add three-dimensional parts to some sections with cut paper. When all students have finished working with paints and paper, put the parts aside to dry. They may be assembled the next day by stacking them in sets of six or eight and securing them with white glue.

Totem poles are a success if each student contributes a unique and colorful part to this group project. Indians are a fascinating subject for most elementary children, and the project is a good chance to learn more about them. This, along with primitive masks in Chapter 8 are good enrichment activities to complement a social studies unit on American Indians.

Chapter 5

Exploring the Possibilities of Paper

TORN PAPER SCENES

Materials needed: 12 × 18″ colored construction paper, assorted large and small colored construction paper scraps, and paste. (See Figure 5-1.)

This activity provides practice in fine motor coordination, eye-hand coordination, translation, generalization, and integration.

Present the challenge to your class of making a cut paper picture without cutting. "We don't always need scissors to shape paper in an interesting way," you begin. "The parts of our picture can be torn from paper quite easily. After all, fingers were invented before scissors!" Show the students how a few simple shapes like a circle, a cone, and a square can be torn from paper scraps with a pleasing soft edge which we couldn't get with scissors.

Figure 5-1

Use student ideas as energizers to help each individual think of a subject. "Let's each make our pictures of something that feels nice and soft. What are some of the softest things that you have touched?" Many will be reminded of a pet at home. Some will think of baby chicks or rabbits seen on a trip to a farm. Others will recall a visit to a petting zoo. Let the students share their thoughts.

Reach every individual by determining that each one has thought of an appropriate subject. Have the children, a few at a time, select some paper, bright scraps, and a piece of 12 × 18" colored construction paper for the background. You are aware of those students that may need more help in thinking of or interpreting an idea. Give them individual help and encouragement.

Appreciate each person's work as torn paper pets appear. They do look soft and furry! Some children may prefer the control of cutting. Help to broaden their appreciation of art products by pointing out the pleasing qualities of torn paper. Showing them interesting effects achieved by other students is a good way to accomplish this. When most of the torn paper pictures have been composed, provide paste for securing parts in place.

Exploring the Possibilities of Paper

Torn paper pictures are a success if your students are able to accept the new way of working with paper. Variety in materials and methods is essential to artistic growth.

INDIAN SHIELDS

Materials needed: 12 × 12" colored construction paper cut on the paper cutter (18 × 24" would be good for older students), scissors, paste, and pictures of Indian art from the "I" encyclopedia or other sources. (See Figure 5-2A.)

Figure 5-2A
Indian Shield

This activity provides practice in fine motor coordination, eye-hand coordination, auditory decoding, translation, organization, generalization, and integration.

Present the challenge to your students of making cut paper designs which imitate the subjects and style of American Indian art. This activity is an enjoyable learning experience at any time

82   Basic Art Skills as Energizers

of the year, but is especially appropriate during the Thanksgiving season when thoughts are focused on Indians and Pilgrims.

Use student ideas as energizers in a discussion of the characteristics of Indian art. Show your students blankets, jewelry, or other examples of Indian-style designs. Your students will observe the triangles, squares, and "zig-zag" lines.

Reach every individual as you give directions. Each student will have paste, scissors, and two pieces of the 12 × 12″ construction paper in contrasting colors. Show the students how to draw a circle within the square by making a curved line from the center of each edge to the center of the next. Working as you talk, cut the circle out and trace it on the second piece of paper. Next, cut out the second circle. Fold it in half, then in quarters. The first circle is the background. The second will be used to make the design by cutting in "zig-zag" lines in an arc across the fold several times. (See Figure 5-2B.) This

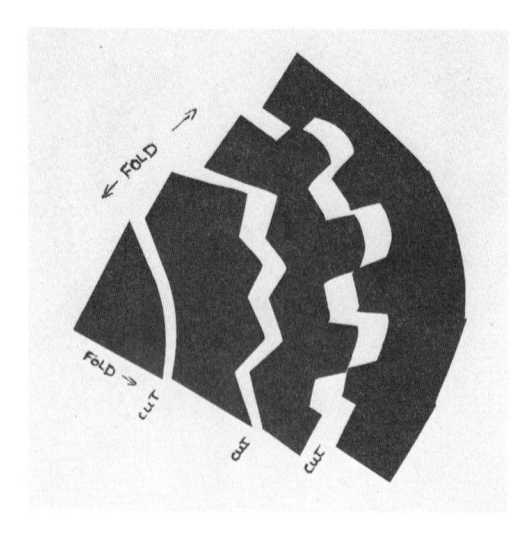

Figure 5-2B

results in concentric circles which are pasted on the background. Explain that only a few of the circular designs should be used or the pattern will be too crowded. Leftovers may be swapped so that each shield has circles of several colors. The shields are completed by pasting a cut paper symbol of something important to the Indian in the center. (See Figure 5-2C.)

Exploring the Possibilities of Paper

Figure 5-2C

Appreciate each person as the class begins to work. You may find that some are disturbed that their circles aren't perfectly round. Point out that the important thing is that both circles are alike in size and shape. As the children complete their shields with a cut paper symbol in the center, remind them that the Indians stylized their drawings, emphasizing the important characteristics of the subject. "Can you do that, too?"

Indian shields are a success if the children are pleased with the bright and striking circular designs. They usually already know quite a lot about Indian art. Through this activity they are able to learn more and produce a product to be proud of.

MOTION MONTAGES

Materials needed: old magazines, 12 × 18″ colored construction paper, paste, and scissors. (See Figure 5-3.)

This activity provides practice in fine motor coordination, eye-hand coordination, translation, organization, generalization, and integration.

Present the challenge to your class of combining a large, colorful magazine picture with cut paper to suggest speed. Ask the children to choose a magazine picture of something that moves quickly.

Figure 5-3
Motion Montage

Use student ideas as energizers while you describe the process. Point out how animated cartoons such as *Charlie Brown* or *Mickey Mouse* are full of action. Younger children will need an explanation of how each character is drawn many times, changing the position of the body slightly in each frame. When these are projected in rapid succession, the character seems to move. This project needs about six identical cut paper shapes.

Reach every individual with a demonstration which will make the directions clear. Cut out the chosen magazine picture and trace it on a piece of 8 × 12" (or smaller) colored construction paper. Place this on top of two more pieces and cut it out. Select two or three other colors of construction paper and repeat. The result will be cut paper silhouettes of the magazine photo. Arrange the parts so that they suggest motion. Overlap the silhouettes on a piece of 12 × 18" colored construction paper, spreading the arrangement over the background and pasting it down. Add the magazine photo. "Doesn't it appear to be moving? Are you ready to set a picture in motion, too?"

Appreciate each person as the children search magazines for something that runs, jumps, or flies. Every selection reflects an individual's interests. Encourage the students to give thought to their compositions, overlapping the parts placed across the paper. Fast pictures are fun!

Exploring the Possibilities of Paper

Motion montages are a success if every child creates the illusion of movement. The project does not depend upon drawing skill. Students learn that overlapping can result in a continuous composition which is very effective. They also discover one way to suggest speed. Have them title their work. Then display the montages and admire the movement.

CREATING DEPTH WITH SIZE AND COLOR

Materials needed: 12 × 18" white drawing paper, 8 × 12" colored construction paper, crayons, paste, and scissors.

This activity provides practice in fine motor coordination, eye-hand coordination, translation, organization, generalization, and integration.

Present the challenge to your artistic individuals of making a cut paper and crayon picture which gives the illusion of depth. "If we touch the surface of a drawing or a painting, it is completely flat," you begin. "Yet some pictures appear to really have depth or distance. Have you ever seen a painting that was so realistic that you felt you could step right into it and walk away?" If possible, show the class an example of a picture that gives the impression of deep space.

Use student ideas as energizers in continuing the discussion. Then ask if students know ways in which artists achieve the effect of depth. They will suggest that objects closest, or in the foreground, are larger, while those farther away, or in the background, are smaller. The closer a color is to us, the brighter it looks. As the sky stretches into the distance and meets the horizon, its color fades. Explain that the class will experiment with size and color to make pictures which appear to have depth.

Reach every individual by encouraging the students to give examples and share ideas about places to see into the distance, such as windows high in a building or the top of a hill. Each boy or girl will choose three things from the scene that they have in mind and will cut them out of paper. The closest object in the scene will be the largest and cut from the brightest colored paper, and placed near the bottom edge of the background paper. The second object will be somewhat smaller, lighter in color, and placed above the first. As you explain, cut out the shapes of a simple scene and arrange them on the background paper. A beach umbrella, a sailboat, and a lighthouse could be

Figure 5-4A

Figure 5-4B

quick and easy. "The last thing that we add will be smallest of all and lightest in color. Crayon detail will complete the project." (See Figures 5-4A, 5-4B, and 5-4C.)

Appreciate each person after paper and paste have been passed out. Most students are all set with an idea and ready to start cutting shapes, but sometimes choosing a subject can be the most difficult part of a project. See that everyone is off to a good start. When the three paper pieces are in place, suggest that students color in the finishing touches.

Exploring the Possibilities of Paper

Figure 5-4C

Creating depth with size and color is a success if the children learn how to achieve the illusion of space—and enjoy doing it. The four step process helps to ensure an attractive picture for each individual.

WALLPAPER STILL LIFES

Materials needed: old wallpaper books, 8 × 12" colored construction paper, construction paper scraps, paste, scissors, crayons, or markers. (See Figure 5-5.)

This activity provides practice in fine motor coordination, eye-hand coordination, translation, organization, and generalization.

Present the challenge to your class of using wallpaper as a background for a still life composition cut from paper. Explain that a still life is a picture of inanimate—not living—objects. Often still life paintings or drawings are of vases of flowers or bowls of fruit because they are bright, attractive, and decorative. Still life sketches are not always pretty. After all, art can be about a subject of personal interest to the artist, whether it is pretty or not!

Use student ideas as energizers by having individuals in the class share thoughts about things which interest them whether, they are beautiful or not. Encourage the children to avoid stereotyped notions of beauty and concentrate on objects which have personal significance to the particular child. The discussion will energize your students until they are eager to

Figure 5-5

    share their suggestions from toys such as rag dolls, stuffed animals, and fire trucks to favorite furnishings like a clock, a bedside lamp, or a hanging planter. Now is the time to provide instructions and materials so that the ideas may be expressed visually with paper.

Reach every individual by making your own wallpaper still life. Explain each step as you work, using a page from an old wallpaper book as a background. Draw and cut out the chosen object on 8 × 12″ colored construction paper. Next, draw and cut out from colored paper scraps two or three other things related to the first. Point out that these favorite things can't be left floating in midair. From a large paper scrap cut out a shelf or a table to place the objects on. All the parts of the still life are then arranged and pasted on the wallpaper background. Overlapping several parts will result in a more pleasing composition. When all students understand the directions, let them select their papers.

Appreciate each person and continue to energize the class as you notice original ideas and share them with all the students. Take the time to give extra help to the slow starters. One may still be having difficulty choosing a subject. Another could have a drawing problem. Lend a hand where needed. Soon

Exploring the Possibilities of Paper

every individual is hard at work. When all parts are pasted in place, details may be added with crayons or markers.

Wallpaper still lifes are a success if nearly all of the subjects chosen are unusual and unique. You can then be sure that your explanation was excellent. Your students are learning that art is more than a pretty picture—it is a personal expression.

DESIGNS WITH REPEATED SHAPES

Materials needed: 12 × 18″ colored construction paper, 4 × 6″ colored construction paper (cut on the paper cutter), paste, scissors and crayons. (See Figure 5-6.)

Figure 5-6

This activity provides practice in fine motor coordination, eye-hand coordination, association, translation, and organization.

Present the challenge to your class of developing a design from a single shape. Show them that designs are often made from shapes that are similar or even identical because the similarity results in an arrangement which has unity—all the parts of the composition seem to belong together. Unity is an important quality in art. We can make designs which have unity by selecting a shape and repeating it many times.

Use student ideas as energizers as you discuss some suitable subjects for shapes. Ask for some things that usually come in groups or bunches. Bunches of bananas, bunnies, and bouquets of flowers may be suggested. Groups of girls, cars in parking lots, and sets of dishes may be mentioned. Compliment the class on their ideas and explain that you are anxious to see their designs!

Reach every individual by directing everyone, step by step. As you talk, you cut and paste. First draw the single shape that you have chosen on a piece of 4 × 6″ colored construction paper. This drawing should be large enough to almost fill the paper. Next take two or three more pieces of the 4 × 6″ paper and, placing the drawing on top of them, cut it out. Presto! Already there are three or four identical shapes. Try arranging them in different ways on the 12 × 18″ background paper. Overlapping some parts adds to the unity and makes the composition more pleasing. Unless the initial drawing was quite big, more shapes will be needed to complete the design. The shape may be traced and the cutting process repeated providing three or four more of the original object.

Appreciate each person and the many amusing ideas which are being expressed as the children work. Admire every student's design. Advise each to experiment with different arrangements of the shapes, adding or removing some before pasting. Remind them not to forget to overlap. Crayon or marker details may be added last of all.

Designs from repeated shapes are a success if no people have problems expressing ideas. Achieving an interesting cut paper shape seems to come naturally to children. Tracing it and cutting more is easy. The resulting designs are colorful and have a pleasant unity. Ask each student to title his work.

TRANSPARENT TISSUE WINDOWS

Materials needed: 12 × 18″ black construction paper (8 × 12″ could be used with younger children), pieces of tissue paper in assorted colors, white glue, and scissors. Pictures of stained glass windows would be helpful, too. (See Figure 5-7A.)

This activity provides practice in fine motor coordination, eye-hand coordination, auditory decoding, translation, and generalization.

Exploring the Possibilities of Paper 91

Figure 5-7A

Present the challenge to your students of using cut paper to create window decorations which give the effect of stained glass. Explain that stained glass is a very old art form used for many centuries. The students may have seen stained glass windows in churches. Today artists are using stained glass for lampshades and other useful and decorative items. Show the students pictures of stained glass work.

Use student ideas as energizers as you explain that paper will be used to make windows that suggest stained glass. Hold a piece of tissue paper up to the light, pointing out that it is transparent. Black construction paper will hold the design together, just as lead holds together the pieces of real stained glass. Point out that most stained glass windows are symmetrical in shape—that is, they are the same on both sides. Traditional windows were often shaped in an arch, either round or pointed. Provide a picture for illustration, if possible. Black construction paper is to be the frame for these windows, and someone will see that it can best be cut into a symmetrical shape by folding it in half! Since you'll need both a front and a back piece to make the decoration attractive from both sides, ask how to get two pieces that are identical. Someone will tell you to fold and cut two pieces of paper at the same time.

Reach every individual by showing the students how the process works. Fold two pieces of black construction paper in half. Cut an arch, starting at the bottom of the open edge and curving up to the top of the fold. Keeping the paper folded, cut a design from the inside of the arch. Do not cut through the outside edge. (See Figures 5-7B, 5-7C, and 5-7D.) Open it so the class may see the results. Demonstrate how pieces of tissue paper may be glued over the open parts of the design on one of the arches. When this is done, the second arch is placed over the first with the tissue paper "sandwich style" in the middle. A simple shape like an arch may serve as a frame, or someone may try something different. You may draw your picture or design with a pencil before cutting. Make sure that you fold your paper so that the frame will be even. Cut both front and back together so that they will be the same.

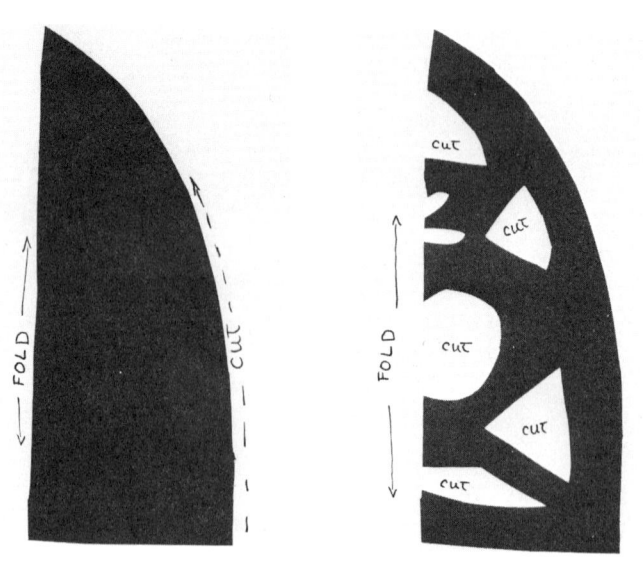

Figure 5-7B   **Figure 5-7C**

Appreciate each person as the designs are planned. Cutting folded paper has a unique fascination for all and functions well as an energizer. As the children work, they discover that a design

Exploring the Possibilities of Paper

cut on one side of the fold becomes two designs when the paper is opened. Or the fold may be the center of one symmetrical design. They are pleased and excited—share their enthusiasm. Help them to avoid a common mistake by reminding them that the fold is the center of the window frame. They must not cut through the open outside edges.

Transparent tissue windows are a success if each child makes a bright, symmetrical decoration. From outside the building they are an attractive window decoration. Inside, they cast colorful prisms of light over the class. The children are often so excited that they ask to make more in their spare time. What more could you ask for?

Figure 5-7D

NEWSPAPER COMPOSITIONS

Materials needed: newspapers, pieces of cloth, scraps of colored construction paper, 12 × 18″ colored construction paper, crayons, scissors, and paste. (See Figure 5-8.)

This activity provides practice in fine motor coordination, eye-hand coordination, auditory decoding, sequencing, association, translation, organization, generalization, and integration.

Present the challenge to children of using collage to make a visual statement about familiar things. You may ask if anyone knows what "collage" means. Although it sounds unusual be-

Figure 5-8

cause it is a French word, it simply means something made by pasting. A collage is a picture or design made from a variety of materials pasted together on a background. The class will make some collages from newspaper, cloth, and construction paper.

Use student ideas as energizers by helping each child choose a subject for his collage. "It might be interesting to make our collages about three things which we see on the way to school. What might some be?" you ask. Many familiar objects will be suggested.

Reach every individual with step-by-step directions. Everyone will need a 12 × 18" sheet of construction paper for the background, a sheet of newspaper, a scrap of construction paper, and a piece of cloth. Starting with the largest of the three objects chosen, draw this on the newspaper and cut it out, making the drawing big enough to take up almost half of the background. Next, draw the medium size object chosen on the construction paper and cut this out. Cut the smallest object from the cloth. Experiment with arrangements of the parts until you and the class settle on the most pleasing one. Overlapping some parts is a good idea. Paste your collage together and add details with crayon or marker.

Exploring the Possibilities of Paper

Appreciate each person as the collages are constructed. The three step process is not complicated. Every child has the experience from which to draw subject material. Most are sure of success, but your compliments are still welcomed by students. You should know which individuals in your class require more encouragement and you should provide it. Confidence is an energizer!

Newspaper compositions are a success if your class learns about collage, expresses a personal idea, and has a good time doing it. Such activities build confidence which is transferred to other academic areas and contributes to a good self-image for each student.

Chapter 6

Interpreting the World with Watercolor

WATERCOLOR WASH: A SPECIAL SKY

Materials needed: 12 × 18″ white drawing paper, 6 × 18″ strips of black construction paper cut on the paper cutter, watercolor paints, 3/4″ easel brushes, water, tissues or paper towels, and glue. (See Figure 6-1A.)

This activity provides practice in fine motor coordination, eye-hand coordination, auditory decoding, association, translation, organization, generalization, and integration.

Present the challenge to each child of mastering a new technique in watercolor painting and applying the skill in making a special picture about the sky. Explain that a watercolor wash is a method which artists often use in beginning a painting. It is a way of creating a broad area of color—the sky or water. It is called a "wash" because the color is actually washed over the painting surface with a brush. It would be interesting to experiment with a watercolor wash as we paint pictures about the sky at sunrise or sunset, you suggest.

98   Basic Art Skills as Energizers

Figure 6-1A

Use student ideas as energizers to help the class give creative consideration to the sky. Discuss how the sky looks when the sun is going down and is pink or golden at the horizon. Overhead it is blue and sometimes clouds pick up the bright colors of the sunset. "Do we see colors other than pink, yellow, and blue at sunrise or sunset? Certainly! The skies are often red, orange, and purple, too. Do you think that we can show this in a painting?"

Reach every individual by showing him a technique that he can use to paint his special picture of the sky. Have your work area covered with newspaper and have paper, a brush, watercolor paints, tissues, and water ready. "First let's put down the blue of the sky overhead." "Load" the brush with water, then rub it on the blue paint. A watercolor wash should not be too dark in color. Starting at the top, brush the paint across the paper and back. If the blue color needs to be darker, dip the brush in the paint again. Wash the color from side to side down the paper. The more you brush, the lighter the color becomes. Stop when you get to the center of the paper. Use a tissue to blot some areas of the sky. This gives the effect of clouds. (See Figure 6-1B.) "Now I will try to show the splen-

Interpreting the World with Watercolor 99

Figure 6-1B

did color of the sunset," you continue. Starting at the bottom edge of the paper and working up, use the same watercolor wash technique with red, orange, or yellow paint. Put some of the sunset colors on the clouds in the blue sky. If they appear too dark, lift a bit of color off with a tissue. Add deeper tones of blue or purple to the sky. Students are motivated to try their own watercolor wash.

Appreciate each person after desks are covered with newspaper and everyone has paper, paints, a brush, tissues or a paper towel, and water. Remind students to put the paint on with long sweeps of the brush and to mingle sunset colors with the blue sky, adding deeper tones as well. "And don't forget to use the tissues if colors are too dark or too wet!" As each child finishes his wash, have him clean his brush, paint tray, and water cup and put them away. He should take a piece of the 6 × 18" black construction paper as he returns to his seat. Pushing his painting to the side of his desk to dry, he may use the black paper to cut a silhouette of something which might be seen on the horizon at sunrise or sunset. The silhouette could be of rolling hills, skyscrapers, rooftops, or treetops. This is glued across the bottom of the paper to complete the picture.

Watercolor wash paintings are a success if learning a new art technique seems to be challenging to the children. The wash of color lends student work a sophistication which they appreciate, and sunrise or sunset is a dramatic subject. The frustration of trying to paint details on a wet picture is avoided by adding cut paper silhouettes, which make the paintings "double-dramatic"!

WAX RESIST PAINTINGS: OUT AT NIGHT

Materials needed: 12 × 18" manila paper, crayons, dark watercolor paints, 3/4" easel brushes, and water. (See Figure 6-2.)

This activity provides practice in fine motor coordination, eye-hand coordination, verbal endings, translation, generalization, and integration.

Figure 6-2

Present the challenge to each child of combining crayons and paint to make a picture about something unusual which happened to him one night. "A lot of exciting things happen at night," you begin. "Perhaps it just seems that way because most of us stay up really late only on special occasions like Halloween, the Fourth of July, or New Year's Eve. Let's each think of a time when we stayed out long after dark having a lot of fun."

Use student ideas as energizers as everyone joins in a class discussion of nights that were especially happy, like a night baseball game, a trip to the stock car races, riding on a snowmobile, camping out, or seeing a fireworks display. Responses will vary according to the age and environment of the group, as well as the personalities of individual children. This is one of the things that makes art so much fun.

Reach every individual by inviting the class to group around you for a demonstration. Your work area is covered with newspaper. Paints, brush, and water are within reach. Using heavy strokes of the crayon, color small areas of the manila paper red, yellow, brown, and black. "What do you suppose will happen if I paint over these colors?" you ask, brushing black watercolor over the paper. "Yes, the paint rolls right off the parts covered with wax crayon. The wax protects the surface from the water. Wax and water won't mix, you point out. "Notice that the brighter colors show up much better than do the brown and black. Try to use many light colors and avoid dark ones in your pictures," you warn. Explain to the class that they will draw about their special nights with crayons. These drawings should be colored in with lots of crayon, making them as bright as possible. When this has been done, black watercolor paint will be brushed over the entire picture.

Appreciate each person as the children begin to color. It is exciting for each child to learn a new technique which he can use to interpret a personal experience. Most students will be anxious to work with the black watercolor. They are intrigued with the way that it seems to disappear when brushed over crayon-colored paper. This is a good energizer, but unless plenty of time is spent on the crayon drawings, the special effect will be lost. Rather than giving paint to every person, you may prefer to set up one area in the room where the painting can be done. Cover a table with newspaper and provide sets of paints and brushes. Have the children go there to finish their pictures when they are done with their crayons.

Wax resist pictures are a success if each child has a special night which he wants to tell about in a picture. Since each student is comfortable with crayons, the pictures are easy to do. Brushing paint over the pictures adds a touch of excitement which the children enjoy. Integrate this activity with your language program by having students write stories about their pictures. A sentence will do for the younger child. Or simply let each one tell the class about one time he stayed up very late!

STAINED GLASS WINDOWS

Materials needed: 12 × 18" white drawing paper, watercolor paints, water, and black crayons. Pictures of stained glass windows are helpful, too. (See Figure 6-3A.)

Figure 6-3A

This activity provides practice in fine motor coordination, eye-hand coordination, translation, organization, generalization, and integration.

Present the challenge to your class of using simple materials to make simulated stained glass windows which symbolize a personal interest. This activity is related to transparent tissue windows, Chapter 5, which differed from this lesson where the windows which result are opaque. The materials used are easy for students to manage, thus allowing a lot of freedom of expression.

Use student ideas as energizers while you show them a few photographs of stained glass windows. Explain that craftsmen and artists have been making these windows for many hundreds of years and that the pieces of glass are held together by black lead. Some windows are in the shape of a curved or pointed arch. Others are round or even square. Many are pictures which tell a story and many are simply designs. Notice that lots of bright colors are used and that the lead work is a very important part of the design.

Reach every individual by explaining how black crayons and watercolors can be used to achieve the effect of stained glass. "First we must think of a picture or design for our windows. Everyone will have his own idea and each window will be

Interpreting the World with Watercolor 103

Figure 6-3B

Figure 6-3C

different," you explain. "I think that I will use a flower." Show the students how to draw the object chosen in the center of the 12 × 18" paper with black crayon. The outline should be simple. Point out to the students that some of the pieces of glass in stained glass windows are not actually parts of the picture, but only decorative colored shapes which add to the design. "We can imitate this by drawing different shapes around the picture in the center. Notice how I keep my hand moving quickly and continuously." (See Figures

Figure 6-3D

6-3B and 6-3C.) "Now the paper is filled with many interesting shapes outlined with crayon. By painting each shape a different color, we can create the effect of stained glass."

Appreciate each person as the children begin their black crayon drawings. Caution them to make the picture in the center quite large and keep their drawing simple. Too many small parts are difficult to paint. As each finishes his crayon sketch, have him decide what shape his window should be. Suggest that the frame repeat the contour of the picture in the center. A pointed arch would be appropriate for a long drawing. Of course, a round picture would fit well in a circle. (See Figure 6-3D.) A curved arch may complement still another drawing. After the paper has been trimmed accordingly with scissors, color may be added to each of the many small sections of the drawing with watercolor paint. The painting will be done more quickly if students use one color at a time on parts all over the picture, rather than changing colors for each successive section.

Watercolor stained glass windows are a success if each one is unique and reflects a personal interest of the students. They could be displayed on separate panes of glass in your classroom windows or, mounted on construction paper, become folders for taking home the week's papers. Also, an unusual display could be made by tacking or stapling them against a black background on your bulletin board.

Interpreting the World with Watercolor

WATERCOLOR PORTRAITS: STORYBOOK PEOPLE

Materials needed: 12 × 18″ white drawing paper, watercolor paints, 3/4″ easel brushes, fine brushes, water, tissues or paper towels. (See Figure 6-4.)

This activity provides practice in fine motor coordination, eye-hand coordination, verbal endings, translation, generalization, and integration.

Figure 6-4

Present the challenge to each child of making a watercolor portrait of one of his favorite storybook characters. Explain that when a story is being read to us or even when reading to ourselves, many pictures are formed in our minds. We imagine how the people and places look. Often an artist illustrates the book with his own interpretation of the setting and characters. Illustrations can be a very important part of a book. Don't we all sometimes choose library books just because of their attractive pictures?

Use student ideas as energizers as you discuss how scenes from the students' favorite books might be illustrated. Ask the students to think of stories that they like a lot and how they imagine the characters in the stories look. Responses are sure to range from fairy tales like *Snow White* to adventure stories

Basic Art Skills as Energizers

like *Robinson Crusoe,* from classics like *Tom Sawyer* to comics like *Charlie Brown,* and from the traditional like *Cinderella* to the contemporary like *The Little Prince.* Point out that illustrations that appear almost real are fun to look at, but they don't have to be like that. Fantastic and imaginative pictures are enjoyable also.

Reach every individual by having him pretend that he is an artist hired to illustrate his favorite book. He is to paint a picture of one of the main characters in a scene from the story. Explain that it is almost impossible to paint light colors over dark, so it must be decided right away which parts of the picture will be white or some light color. Paint these areas in first and let them dry before adding details. Use a flat wide brush in the beginning. Suggest that the students continue painting in broad areas, working from light to dark. Black should be used sparingly. (See Figure 6-5.) When this has been done and

Figure 6-5

Interpreting the World with Watercolor

allowed to dry, small brushes may be used for details. Show how the small brush, when dipped in water and gently turned in the paint, will come to a point. Have several students help pass the paints, brushes, water, and paper. Paper towels or tissues are handy, too.

Appreciate each person, reminding the children that light areas are to be put down first. Urge them to start by using the easel brush. Children are often reluctant to try a wide brush, feeling more in control of a small one. If necessary, demonstrate how the easel brush is more effective for broad areas of color. Students frequently approach painting as they do drawing, by outlining. Painting in whole parts of the picture is a different approach for many. You will find that extra encouragement helps when trying something new. "Wait until the paint has dried before adding details," you caution. "And tissues or towels are good for blotting up puddles of paint or water on your picture."

Story book watercolor portraits are a success if the children welcome an opportunity to paint their favorite characters and learn more about watercolor paints. Trim the edges of the paintings on the paper cutter and have the students mount them on colored construction paper. The title of each book chosen, a sentence describing the scene, and the child's name could be written on a 3 × 5″ piece of paper and attached to the painting. These would be an attractive display for the school library!

WORKING ON WET PAPER: A RAIN FOREST

Materials needed: 12 × 18″ manila paper, 3/4″ easel brushes, fine brushes, watercolor paints, water, tissues or paper towels. (See Figure 6-6A.)

This activity provides practice in fine motor coordination, eye-hand coordination, auditory decoding, translation, association, organization, generalization, and integration.

Present the challenge to the class of using a lot of imagination and a little paint to portray the lush green foliage of a rain forest. Explain that rain forests grow in climates where there are frequent rains. Because of the moisture, rich earth, and warm sun, the trees, flowers, and underbrush are strong and plentiful. Some groups may have studied rain forests in geography units.

Figure 6-6A

Use student ideas as energizers in helping each child form a picture of a rain forest in his mind. Ask what colors would be found in a rain forest and what types of plants would be seen. "Certainly we would see tall trees, leafy undergrowth, and vines in many shades of green. Flowers bloom in lots of vibrant colors. Today we are going to try to capture the effect of a rain forest on paper by using watercolors in a new way."

Reach every individual by demonstrating how to use paint on wet paper. "Just as rain forests grow from moist earth, our painting will be developed on wet paper," you explain. Have the children gather around your work area so that each can see. First use a large brush to apply water over the entire paper. Next work with light colors—yellow, orange, or light red. These will be blossoms. Working quickly with the large brush, paint several areas of color on the paper. "I can put these colors anywhere that I think they would look good because I am using my imagination," you point out. Brush some blue across the top of the paper for sky. A touch of yellow will spread out to suggest the warmth of the sun. Next, before the paper dries, brush on dark green or brown in vertical strokes. These are tree trunks. Have the students notice the interesting shapes that appear as the paint spreads out. New colors have also been created where two colors met. (See Figure

Interpreting the World with Watercolor 109

Figure 6-6B

6-6B.) Now, using a smaller brush, details may be added. Leaves can be outlined, more color painted on the blossoms, and vines drawn. The paint should be thicker and less diluted with water. Blue will darken green, yellow will lighten it. There are many shades of green in a rain forest.

Appreciate each person by providing help where needed. "Don't get your paper too wet," you warn. "There should be no puddles of water. These can be brushed off your paper onto the newspaper over your desk." Remind the children to work very quickly with the large brush first, starting with light colors. More time may be taken with the final details and the small brush later. The shapes made by the paints as they spread out on the paper will often provide ideas for a picture suggesting a flower, a bush, or a vine. A towel or tissue may be used like a blotter if a painting becomes too wet. The watercolors are working for us in this type of painting. Instead of struggling to keep the paints from spreading and running, those qualities are being used to good advantage.

Working on wet paper is a success if your students grow in their understanding and appreciation of watercolor. They experiment with a new way of working, creating colorful and imaginative paintings. Such experiences are essential to the artistic growth of each individual. Keep up the good work!

PAINTING FROM LIFE WITH WATERCOLORS

Materials needed: 12 × 18" white drawing paper, watercolor paints, 3/4" easel brushes, water, crayons, and three or four still life objects. (See Figure 6-7.)

This activity provides practice in fine motor coordination, eye-hand coordination, translation, generalization, and integration.

Present the challenge to your students by showing them several interesting objects which they might enjoy painting. Explain that painting from life means looking carefully at something, then painting it as we see it. Such a painting may be a landscape done outdoors, a portrait of a person, or a still life of interesting things.

Use student ideas as energizers as you set up the still life and discuss the composition, arranging the objects so that some are in front of others. "How could this be shown in a painting? Yes, by overlapping! Overlapping helps to make a picture more pleasing. Each part seems to belong with the others, rather than looking like separate drawings done on the same paper," you observe. Point out that when details are added to a wet painting, the colors run together. That is why artists

Figure 6-7

Interpreting the World with Watercolor

often take many days to complete watercolor work. They wait for their work to dry before painting new parts. "We don't have that much time, so we will draw the picture in detail with crayon first and then paint over it," you explain. "The crayon drawing will show through the paint, since wax and water don't mix."

Reach every individual as you help your class organize for the activity. Desks are covered with newspaper and the paper for painting is passed out. One of the still life objects should be large and placed towards the back of the arrangement, with the others to the side and in front of it. Suggest that the students begin their drawings by lightly sketching in the shape of the largest object. It should almost fill their papers. Ask them to notice the size of the other objects in relation to the large one. That will help them in determining correct proportions in their drawings. Point out that things closest to them should be drawn nearer to the bottom of the paper, overlapping the objects behind. Advise them to use only two crayons for their drawing, a light one such as yellow or white and a dark one like black or brown. Color will be added later with watercolors. Suggest that the pictures be drawn lightly first, the lines darkened as each student is satisfied with his sketch.

Appreciate each person as the drawings are developed. "Your work is good, but quite small," you warn one child. "You will have trouble in drawing details and painting. See if you can do the same good drawing larger!" Another student complains that his picture is too large for the paper. "It's perfectly all right to omit parts which stretch off the paper. That can give your painting more individuality," you point out. As drawings are completed, brushes, paints, and water can be passed out. It is best to wait until this point. Children can be confused by too many materials at a time. It is also tempting to use the paint too soon. "Be sure that all the details you wish to include are drawn with crayons before you begin to paint," you warn them. "And don't apply the paint too heavily or your fine drawings will not show as well!"

Still life watercolors with crayon are a success if most students understand the process and complete a painting. Younger children feel proud at having participated in a grown-up activity like life drawing. Older students are stimulated by the challenge and are happy with their artistic accomplishment.

Keeping Up the Good Work of Building Art Skills

The preceeding activities can be but a beginning for you and your students. Through the lessons, individuals discover that there are many ways to use basic materials. Vary the lessons simply by changing the topics. Thus seasonal interests or units in langauge, social studies, or geography become motivators in keeping up the good work!

A demonstration while introducing an activity is a dependable energizer. Try the project yourself before presenting it as a lesson so that you can anticipate problems or modify directions. The children may attempt to copy you so emphasize that you are showing them only one of many approaches they can use to express their own ideas. Tape the paper to the blackboard as you demonstrate so that each child can see from his seat. Use loops of masking tape instead of paste to secure parts of cut paper projects during your demonstration. It's quicker and cleaner. You may prefer to prepare in advance several examples which show successive steps. Don't be too self-conscious about your artistic ability, though. You are trying to encourage freedom of expression in your students. Be a brave example!

It may be helpful to you, as you keep up the good work of building art skills, to keep newspapers for covering work areas, egg cartons, paper cups, and margarine tubs on hand. Halves of egg cartons are good for tempera paint sharing, since they hold six colors and can be discarded. Paper cups can hold wash water for paint brushes. But if students work from light to dark, no water is needed as brushes may be wiped clean on paper towels. Three-quarter inch easel brushes are best for both tempera and watercolor paints. Small ones should be available but used last!

Speaking of tempera paints, they have been suggested for all printing projects because printing ink, inking trays, and brayers are not always available, but if you have them use them—the results will be more precise. Crayons may also be used to print prepared surfaces by rubbing. This may be more satisfactory for younger classes. Any of the printing activities may be applied when many copies of art work are required for holiday greetings, invitations, announcements, or program covers.

Keep up the good work of learning about color by using chalks or pastels. These can be easier to manage than paints. Spraying with fixative prevents smudging (hair spray works, too). Working on wet paper lends a special effect. Oil pastels are brighter and not powdery. If your budget allows, try them!

Paper cutting is an especially enjoyable activity. In addition to the lessons suggested, keep up the good work by having each child cut the letters of his name from colored paper, then use them in a design. Folding and cutting paper into lacy designs is always fun and expanded cutting is interesting. Shapes are repeatedly cut and folded out from a piece of paper, then pasted on a large background. Positive and negative shapes are good energizers, too. An object's outline is drawn on 8 × 12" paper and cut out. Both the shape and the scrap paper are mounted on 12 × 18" paper. Cut geometric shapes from colored construction paper to make designs. Or make paper mosaics by drawing a large shape, cutting it out, then cutting it into fragments and pasting it on a contrasting background—one piece at a time.

Paper is a quick and easy sculpting material, too, as it can be folded and then cut into various figures that can stand. Two other good sculpting materials are salt and starch. One quart salt, two cups starch, and three cups water cooked until thick will provide an average class with a handful each. Paint completes the mini-sculptures. And speaking of materials that come from the kitchen, gadgets such as potato mashers, pot scrubbers, jar lids, and tubes inside of paper towels—to name a few—are fun to paint and print.

Keeping Up the Good Work of Building Art Skills

In presenting these activities, as in teaching any lesson, relating new information to previous learning helps make the experience meaningful. As a teacher you know that mastering a process or an approach can be as important as the product. And pleasure creates a positive attitude. So keep up the good work and have fun!

PART 2

Imagination and Environment as Energizers

This part of the book introduces activities which complement the skill building lessons found in the first section. In a good art program it is important to balance projects which emphasize skills with those that focus on personal expression. Each child's imagination is an excellent energizer in such lessons.

Some of the lessons present unusual topics which will draw interesting responses and encourage free expression, helping to avoid tight, stereotyped use of materials. Children's interest and enthusiasm are sustained and artistic growth assured. Introducing the imagination as an energizer also enables you to present the maturing child with more complex ideas. The young child is best motivated with simple ideas involving his relationship to his surroundings, but the older child requires more challenging topics. In addition to providing the stimulation of fantasy, the activities lead students to new uses of ordinary materials, which is as important to continued interest as new ideas!

The chapter on puppet making uses children's love for drama as an energizer. Creating and using puppets encourages clear speech, helps the child project himself unselfconsciously, and increases skills of perception and concept forming. Making masks also capitalizes on the child's flair for the dramatic. Characters represented by masks perform incidents from stories, songs, or poems, or the students themselves become authors of plays as part of your language program. Such activities are ideal for small groups of children working independently or an individualized classroom, and also have an important place in a traditional setting. Another chapter leads students into a whole new world where images are drawn from fantasy. Individuality is emphasized with each child's personal and unique response.

Personal response to the environment is the other energizer in the chapters which follow. One of the primary functions of an art program is to aid the child in understanding his environment and his relationship to it. Thus direct experiences with aspects of the environment are the basis for challenging art activities. As each child discusses his experience, he learns more about himself and gains confidence as an individual—he discovers that his response is often unique and sometimes universal. At the same time, his appreciation for others increases while he learns to listen and value other contributions. Direct experience also stimulates the child to learn more about a particular topic and to turn to additional sources of information.

The individualized awareness activities encourage students to become more sensitive and observant. Some of them may be used as a prelude or follow-up to lessons in science or reading. The mini-excursions enable children to take a new look at the familiar, and typically result in art work unusually clear in detail. Describing experiences visually depends on an individual's recalling them orally first. This practice builds the verbal skills needed to succeed not only in school but in life.

Use these lessons with the understanding that individuals in your class are at varying levels of artistic growth. Be accepting and appreciative of each expression, simple or sophisticated, and each student will enjoy himself as he learns and grows. So will you!

Chapter 7

Creative Play and Dramatics with Puppets

PAPER BAG PUPPET PALS

Materials needed: brown paper lunch bags, yarn, cloth and colored paper scraps, glue, and scissors. (See Figure 7-1A.)

This activity provides practice in fine motor coordination, eye-hand coordination, auditory decoding, verbal endings, translation, organization, generalization, and integration.

Present the challenge to each child in your class of turning a paper bag into a puppet playmate. "It's really fun to have a friend," you begin. "A friend is someone to talk to, someone to share secrets with, and someone with whom to make special plans. This friend might be a boy or girl, a favorite animal, or a secret friend that lives just in our imagination!"

Use student ideas as energizers by showing the children how to transform a paper bag into a special friend. Slip your hand inside the partly folded bag. The bottom of the bag will be the puppet's face. "What will we need first to give our puppet personality?" you ask. (See Figure 7-1B.) "Sure! Eyes are

120 **Imagination and Environment as Energizers**

Figure 7-1B
Paper Bag Puppet Pal

very important. They should be big and bright!" Working with scissors as you talk, cut and paste on paper scrap eyes. "What other features does our pal need?" you continue. "Of course! If he is to talk with us, he needs a mouth! If we put his top lip on the lower folded edge of the bottom of the bag, he will be able to open and close his mouth!" The students will be amused as you demonstrate. Paste the mouth on in two

Creative Play and Dramatics with Puppets

pieces, then with your hand curved inside the bag and your fingertips against the fold, open and close your hand. The puppet appears to be talking! Ears and a nose can be made from paper. Yarn would be good for the hair.

Reach every individual as you encourage the class to use imagination. "Each of you is a special person. No other student here is exactly like you. Therefore, each of you should have a puppet pal that is different from all the others!" Give each child a paper bag, scissors, and glue. Then let them all select paper scraps and yarn to get started. Suggest that the cloth scraps be used to make clothes for the body of the puppet and fancy touches like collars and neckties.

Appreciate each person by providing a time for sharing when the puppets are complete. Have every child give his "playmate" a name. Then, one by one, the students can introduce their pals to the class. It would be fun to hear each puppet tell a few interesting things about himself!

Puppet pals are a success if your children actively take up the idea of a puppet friend, and they enjoy using their imaginations in making them. Time for sharing can become a mini-lesson in manners as proper introductions are practiced. The puppet pals turn out to be friends, indeed, who help everyone have fun with language!

STOCKING HAND PUPPETS

Materials needed: clean but discarded old stockings, buttons, cloth and yarn scraps, scissors, and glue. Corchet hooks and needles with large eyes are helpful, too. (See Figure 7-2A.)

This activity provides practice in fine motor coordination, eye-hand coordination, auditory decoding, translation, organization, generalization, and integration.

Present the challenge to children of raiding a rag bag to find parts for a puppet. Have each child bring a clean old sock, buttons, and cloth and yarn scraps from home. Ask students to also bring along needles with large eyes and crochet hooks if they can. A few of these should be available for the group to share. "A lot of fun can be had with things that have been thrown away," you observe, holding up a sock. "For example, with a little imagination, we could make a sock into a puppet!"

Use student ideas as energizers while you pull the stocking over your hand. The top of your wrist should be at the heel of the

Figure 7-2A
Stocking Hand Puppet

sock. Push the toe inside out towards the palm of your hand, between your fingers and thumb. Right away the children will see the possibilities! What a good energizer! "What sort of creatures could evolve from a stocking?" you ask. "Yes, surely something with a long neck, flat face, and huge mouth! A sea serpent? Perhaps! A snake? A dragon? A frog?" (See Figure 7-2B.)

Reach every individual by explaining that mouths can be important parts of puppets. A mouth that moves makes the puppet appear to really be talking. These sock puppets will all have huge mouths. That's a good place to begin! Show the children how to cut an oval from a scrap of cloth and place it inside the toe—or puppet's mouth. A bright cloth scrap tongue may be inserted also or cloth teeth attached around the edge. Felt scraps, being fairly stiff, would make good incisors. Buttons make good eyes and show up better if they are put on colorful cloth circles. The eyes, of course, should be located under the heel of the sock, or on top of your hand just below the wrist. Eyelashes, ears, nostrils, and other details may be cut from

Figure 7-2B
Stocking Hand Puppet

cloth scraps and added. Yarn is good for manes or hair. White glue may be used to attach all parts to the puppet. If needles are available, however, you may prefer to have your students sew their puppets together. Sewing is good for coordination as well as being a useful skill that many children have no chance to learn. It takes more time, but the puppets will last longer. Crochet hooks can be used to pull strands of yarn through the sock for hair. Once started, this could be a project for students to pick up when work is done. As such, it complements an individualized curriculum.

Appreciate each person if every child seems anxious to "show off" his accomplishment. Use this as an energizer in language arts. Let the students form small groups and present puppet plays. These should be short and spontaneous. If you let two groups of three children give a performance each day, within a week everyone will have had a turn.

Stocking hand puppets are a success if the children show they enjoy the challenge and the novelty of working with cloth. If you take the time to help them with sewing, your efforts and theirs are most rewarding. And if just glue is used, it is fun, too! The puppet plays are entertaining and for once, "showing off" is a good way to act!

PAPIER-MÂCHÉ AND CLOTH HAND PUPPETS

Materials needed: inch wide strips of oak tag, masking tape, wheat paste, water, containers, newspapers, tempera paints, brushes, and large cloth scraps. (See Figure 7-3A.)

This activity provides practice in fine motor coordination, eye-hand coordination, auditory decoding, verbal endings, translation, organization, generalization, and integration.

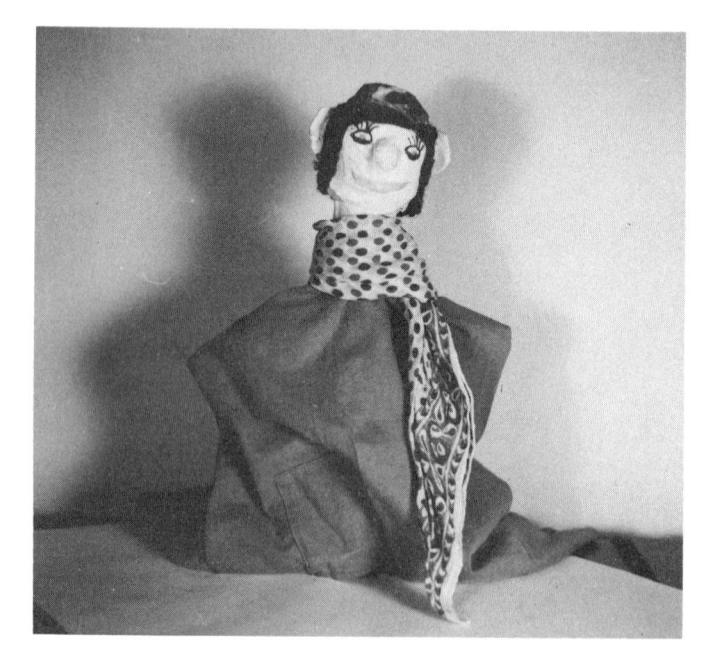

Figure 7-3A
Papier-Mâché Puppet Head

Present the challenge to your students of adding sizeable amounts of time, effort, and imagination to basic art materials in order to produce some durable and personable puppets perfect for classroom performances. If your class had no previous experience with papier-mâché, introduce them to the media. (See Chapter 4.) Explain that papier-mâché is a sculpting material consisting of newspaper moistened with wheat paste. When it dries, it becomes nearly as hard as wood and can be painted. It is quite permanent and is excellent for puppet making. Most papier-mâché projects are done in several steps and require two or three weeks to complete.

Use student ideas as energizers as you further explain and demonstrate the process. Have your work area covered with news-

Creative Play and Dramatics with Puppets 125

paper and a can of wheat paste mixed with water ready. Also have handy scraps of newspaper torn into pieces, several strips of masking tape, and an inch wide piece of oak tag. "Just the heads of our puppets will be made from papier-mâché," you begin. "What shape will we need to start with? Right, one that is round or oval!" Crumple several pieces of newspaper into a ball and secure the shape by wrapping it with a couple of lengths of masking tape. (See Figure 7-3B.) Next a place to fit fingers is needed. Use a strip of oak tag for this. Curl the oak tag into a cylinder which fits around your first three fingers. Wrap it with masking tape. Now attach the cylinder to the newspaper ball with a strip of tape which extends from one side of the cylinder up over the top and down the other side. This base will be covered with a layer of papier-mâché. When this dries, noses, ears, and other details will be added. Provide your class with newspaper, tape, and oak tag strips. Repeat the instructions as students assemble the bases.

Figure 7-3B
Papier-Mâché Puppet Head

Reach every individual when the first step has been done by showing your students how to dip a scrap of newspaper in the wheat paste and pull it out between thumb and forefinger in order to remove excess moisture. Next smooth it over the newspaper base and continue the process until the form is covered with a layer of papier-mâché. Emphasize that the surface should be as wrinkle free as possible. Push desks into several newspaper-covered groups. Provide cans of paste and piles of newspaper at each station. Every child can cover his base with a layer of papier-mâché. These are put to dry in an out-of-the-way area of your room. Facial features will be added later. Directions are found in Chapter 4, lesson 2.

Appreciate each person as paint and cloth are added to the puppets and everyone enjoys the dramatic transformation. First, tempera colors must be used with care. Again group the desks for sharing and cover them with newspaper. Egg cartons are good paint containers—half of one for each group. Each child should have a brush and a paper towel. Simple paint jobs are usually most effective. Suggest that children begin with a large brush to paint the entire face and back of the head the desired color or colors. When this is dry, features may be painted on in contrasting colors with a smaller brush.

Papier-mâché hand puppets are a success if students show that they are delighted with the results. The final step is simply draping a large cloth scrap over the hand and gluing it inside the cylinder neck. A collar or necktie may be fastened around the neck and a hat or yarn hair placed atop the head. Devote a language lesson to writing plays, construct a puppet theater from an old refrigerator carton, and invite others in the school to the production. Everyone should share the fun!

STUFFED STORYBOOK PUPPETS

Materials needed: 12 × 18" colored construction paper, crayons, scissors, glue, cloth and paper scraps, staplers and staples, newspaper, and dowels, rulers, or other suitable sticks. (See Figure 7-4.)

This activity provides practice in fine motor coordination, eye-hand coordination, auditory decoding, verbal endings, translation, organization, generalization, and integration.

Present the challenge to each student of bringing to life through puppetry a favorite storybook character. Reading is the energizer in this activity! Have every child select a recently read story and from this choose the character which he found most appealing. It will be exciting to see these ideas turned into puppets!

Use student ideas as energizers during a lively class discussion. "What character did you choose and why?" you ask. The children respond with interest and enthusiasm. Help each to conceptualize the character chosen by having outstanding fea-

Creative Play and Dramatics with Puppets 127

Figure 7-4
Stuffed Paper Storybook Puppet

tures described. This will encourage individuals to include unique details and result in lively looking puppets. You may discover that some children want to organize into groups, each making a different character from the same story.

Reach every individual by explaining that everyone has two pieces of 12 × 18" colored construction paper. The chosen character should be drawn on that paper, large enough to reach out to the edges all around. Long, thin parts should be avoided, since the puppet must be plump enough to stuff. Suggest that the character be drawn dressed in clothes with wide sleeves and trouser legs or in a gown with a full skirt. When most students are done with the drawings, have them hold both pieces of paper together and cut the figures out. This produces both front and back of the puppets! At this point some students can start working with staplers. The staples should be about half an inch in from the edge of the paper and an inch apart all around the edge of the puppet. A six inch opening should be left for inserting the newspaper stuffing. As some staple, others can be drawing and brightly coloring in the features of the puppet faces and details of the clothing, both front and back. Cloth or yarn scraps may also be used if desired.

Appreciate each person as the crayon and cloth details are added. Be sure that everyone has worked hard with his crayons. Each puppet's features should be bright and dramatic, even from a distance. The puppets are now ready to be stuffed. Hand-sized pieces of newspaper should be torn, crumpled, and gently pushed through the opening in the puppet's side. The puppet must be firm but not filled to bursting! Staple the opening closed and push a stick such as a ruler or dowel up between the staples at the bottom of the puppet. That becomes a handle. The storybook characters are set to perform!

Stuffed paper puppets are a success if each one portrays a storybook personality. The puppets should be quite large and show up well. Wouldn't it be fun to use these characters in oral book reports?

CLAY, CLOTH, AND POPSICLE STICK PUPPETS

Materials needed: modeling clay, scraps of cloth, Popsicle sticks, and glue. (See Figure 7-5.)

This activity provides practice in fine motor coordination, eye-hand coordination, auditory decoding, translation, organization, generalization, and integration.

Present the challenge to your potential puppeteers of combining several simple materials to make an amusing mini-puppet. Explain that puppets come in all shapes and sizes, and a little puppet can be as much fun as a large one. Puppets may also be made from many different materials. Collect some clay, cloth scraps, Popsicle sticks, and glue.

Use student ideas as energizers by asking, "What do you think would be the best way to use these materials in puppet making?" Students will see that the clay is perfect for the head because it is very pliable and will be good for modeling the features of faces! Each student should start with a piece the size and shape of an egg. Popsicle sticks become the body, and adding clay makes it fatter. The cloth can be used for clothes.

Reach every individual by providing each one with clay and Popsicle sticks. The children can select their own cloth scraps. Modeling with clay is always stimulating for students. Point out that the more that clay is handled, the easier it becomes to

Figure 7-5
Clay, Cloth, and Popsicle Stick Puppets

manipulate. The warmth of the hands softens it. The Popsicle sticks or pencil points can be used to carve details into the clay. Noses and ears may be pinched and pulled into shape. If self-hardening clay is available, use it instead of modeling clay. The puppets will then be permanent and can be painted.

Appreciate each person as the puppets take shape. Every one is as much an individual as the child who made it! A Popsicle stick stuck into the clay becomes the backbone of the body. A second stick, glued across the first, suggests wide-spread arms. Adding clay to the stick skeletons gives them more substance. Last of all, bright scraps of cloth are draped and twisted over the puppets, creating colorful costumes.

Clay, cloth, and Popsicle stick puppets are a success if the children use them in imaginative play. Any elementary age group will find this unusual combination of materials both an energizer and easy to work with. A stage is easy to make, too. Each student can draw his scenery on 18 × 24" paper and tape it to a wall behind a table or desk. The table is covered with a cloth to hide puppeteers who kneel behind it. And the puppets hold forth, front stage and center!

FOLDED PAPER CREATURES

Materials needed: 8 × 12" paper, paper and cloth scraps, glue, and scissors. (See Figure 7-6A.)

This activity provides practice in fine motor coordination, eye-hand coordination, auditory decoding, visual memory, translation, organization, and generalization.

Figure 7-6A
Folded Paper Creature

Present the challenge to your students of taking a fold of paper and a twist of cloth and coming up with a comical and colorful character. "There are times when it is good to know how to make a quick and easy puppet," you begin, "like when you want to have a puppet show for the fun of it, or you have just read a terrific book or written a story and would like to share it with others through puppetry. We are going to make some 'finished fast' puppets today. The outstanding characteristic of each will be its huge mouth!"

Use student ideas as energizers as you discuss which creatures have the biggest mouths. Children will observe that ducks and geese and other birds with large bills have big mouths

Creative Play and Dramatics with Puppets   131

and baby birds are almost all mouth! Frogs and fish have big mouths and so do dogs when they are barking, lions when they are roaring, or even cows when they are mooing. People can be very "mouthy", too!

Reach every individual with step-by-step directions. Fold the 8 × 12″ paper into three equal sections the long way to demonstrate. Next, fold this in two. Finally, fold each end back so that the edges meet the fold in the center. (See Figure 7-6B.) Put a large cloth scrap over your hand, then put three fingers in one end of the folded paper and your thumb and little finger in the other end. Presto! A puppet with a big mouth all ready to have special details like eyes, nose, hair, ears, teeth, and tongue added!

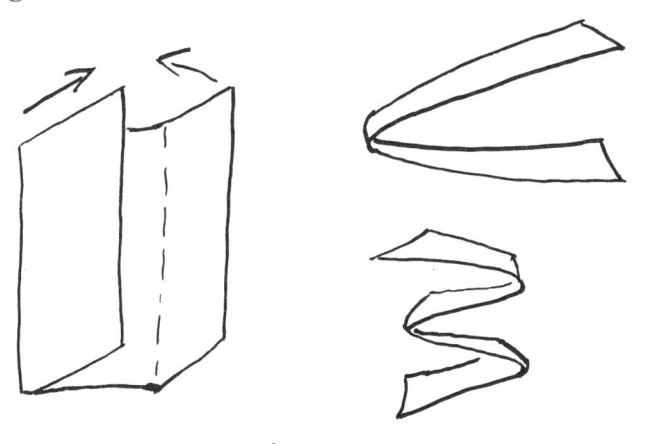

Figure 7-6B

Appreciate each person as the fun begins and students work with scissors, paste, and paper, giving every creature unique and amusing features. Adding lips, teeth, or tongues are ways to make the puppet's huge mouth more important and interesting. Big eyes add expression to the face and big ears can be just the right touch for some characters. The cloth scrap chosen to complete the puppet should complement the creature. And your compliments complete the project!

Folded paper creatures are a success if your students show they are anxious to make more quick and easy puppets during their spare time and at home. Use this enthusiasm as an energizer for your reading and language arts programs. A cardboard carton with part of the bottom cut away and curtains added can be placed on its side on a desk for a stage. You will want to be ready for your puppeteers and their mouthy puppets!

SAWDUST FINGER PUPPETS

Materials needed: tempera paints, brushes, cloth scraps and, for a class of about 25 students, one gallon of sawdust, two quarts of wheat paste, two cups plaster of paris, and enough water to moisten these ingredients. (See Figure 7-7.)

This activity provides practice in fine motor coordination, eye-hand coordination, auditory decoding, translation, and generalization.

Figure 7-7
Sawdust Finger Puppet

Present the challenge to your class of using (of all things) sawdust as the basis of a puppet attractive and durable enough for professional performances. "Any material that can be modeled is good for a puppet head," you begin. "But a modeling material that can be used quickly, can be painted, and is permanent is especially appropriate. Would you believe sawdust?"

Use student ideas as energizers as you mix together the first four ingredients. Discuss possible puppet characters. Stir your recipe well, then give each student a generous half-cup helping to knead until smooth and pliable.

Creative Play and Dramatics with Puppets 133

Reach every individual by suggesting that each knead the mixture until it is smooth, then shape it onto a ball or an oval. With thumb or fingers, make a hole at the base of the head. That enables the puppet to fit on the hand when it is done. Explain that each student must decide if his puppet should have a long nose or a little one, big ears or small ones. He can pinch and pull the material, much as you do clay. Pencils come in handy as etching tools. When they are done, the puppets are put on a shelf to dry. It will probably take a week.

Appreciate each person when the puppet heads have dried and it is time to add the final details. Explain that the puppet heads can be left as is, for the color and texture are pleasing. Important features could be painted with bright tempera colors. Some students may prefer to paint the entire head a different color. That provides opportunity for an individual approach. Set up several paint stations in the room. Children can share materials there—brushes, towels, and paint dispensed in halves of egg cartons. Have each student select a large colorful scrap of cloth. The center of this scrap is glued inside the hole at the base of the puppet's head. Draped over the puppeteer's hand, it becomes the puppet's body.

Sawdust finger puppets are a success if students find the new sculpting material stimulating. If you wish, take the time to make finished looking bodies for the puppets. Have each child cut a paper pattern from a tracing of his hand. Use the patterns to cut both the front and back of the puppets' bodies, then glue or sew them together. The completed heads may be shellacked. Curtain time!

Chapter 8

Mask Making Magic

PAPER PLATE MASKS

Materials needed: a paper plate for each child, 8 × 12″ colored construction paper, colored paper scraps, bits of yarn, scissors, and white glue. (See Figure 8-1.)

This activity provides practice in fine motor coordination, eye-hand coordination, translation, organization, generalization, and integration.

Present the challenge to children in your class of using a paper plate to make a really different dish. "I have a paper plate for each of you," you tell the students. "And I have a recipe for something special to put on the plate! The ingredients are a few paper scraps, a bit of glue, and lots of imagination. I'll supply the first two items. You will have to come up with the third." That introduction should stir up a lot of interest!

Use student ideas as energizers while you explain the project. "We are going to 'cook up' some masks," you continue. "Each mask

Figure 8-1
Pie Plate Mask

will be of a person who has to wear a particular hat because of his job. The paper plate will be the person's face. We will use construction paper and cloth for the hats. Can you think of some people who wear special hats? The class is energized and ready to respond with answers which include baseball players and firemen, policemen and farmers, nurses and queens, and even witches!

Reach every individual with just enough direction to get each student started. Paper plate masks may be made as wall decorations or may be worn. If the children intend to wear their masks, holes must be cut for the eyes. Have every child press the plate gently against his face and mark the places over his eyes lightly with a crayon or a pencil. Next, openings are cut there, so that the child can see through his mask. Younger groups may need your help during this first step. If the masks are for display only, the eyes may be cut and pasted on from colored paper scraps.

Appreciate each person after the materials for features have been selected, imagination added, and the children begin cutting and pasting. Show students how eyes, ears, or other features

Mask Making Magic

which come in pairs may be made identical in size and shape by folding a piece of paper in two or by using two pieces of paper. One ear, for example, is drawn on the top piece. Both pieces of paper are placed together as the ear is cut out. Presto! Two from one! Paper or yarn hair frames the face. The paper hat cut from 8 × 12" colored construction paper atop each mask should be large and include the interesting details which make it special.

Paper plate masks are a success if "cooking something up" with a paper plate is a new approach which the students enjoy. Adding hats is a good energizer. The completed masks can be glued to 12 × 18" colored construction paper backgrounds or tacked to your bulletin board for an unusual and amusing display. If the children are going to wear the masks, use a paper punch on each side and provide a length of string. Won't mother be surprised when her child comes home!

PAPER BAG MASKS

Materials needed: paper bags large enough to cover the head of a child, colored paper and cloth scraps, scissors, and glue. (See Figure 8-2A.)

Figure 8-2A
Huge Paper Bag Masks

This activity provides practice in fine motor corrdination, eye-hand coordination, translation, organization, generalization, and integration.

Present the challenge to each child of turning himself into a fantastic character with the help of his imagination and a paper bag. "Every one of us has pretended that he is someone or something else," you begin. "It is a lot of fun to make believe! Let's use paper bags to help us become a different character for a little while."

Use student ideas as energizers as the class considers how the bags can be made into masks. "The bag will be put over our heads," you explain. "What will we need to do first in order to wear the mask? Of course! We must be able to see where we are going." First the bag should be fitted properly to the head. In most cases it is too tall, so half circles are cut in each side of the bag so that it will fit over the shoulders. (See Figure 8-2B.) Show the children how they can help each other find the right place to put eye holes. One child slips the bag on his head. Another child, very gently, locates his friend's nose and marks a spot on either side with a crayon. Circles, slits, or whatever eye shape is chosen will be cut on these two marks after the bag is removed. The rest of the features will be cut from paper scraps. Yarn and cloth can be hair and clothing.

Reach every individual by giving each child a paper bag and closely supervising the proceedings. Warn the students to use a gentle helping hand when locating their friends' eyes. It would surely spoil the fun if someone was hurt. As each child completes the custom-cutting on his bag, have him get whatever cloth and paper scraps he needs.

Appreciate each person as the paper fantasies are finished. Some children will want to do additional cutting on the bag so that mouths or noses are open, too. Those openings should be decorated with colored paper so that they will show up well. Small squares of white paper make good teeth for a broad smile. Long eyelashes accent a pretty face, heavy brows a severe one. Rosy cheeks can be cut from red paper. Ears should be placed on either side of the head, or even on top! Why not add yarn hair and button or shiny paper earrings? Or perhaps a mustache would be appropriate! Such details create an interesting personality for the pretend person. Cloth collars or cravats complete the character.

Mask Making Magic 139

Figure 8-2B
Huge Paper Bag Masks

Paper bag masks are a success if making the masks is fun and your students delight in wearing them! Let the children put on their masks for a colorful parade of characters around the classroom. Or, if some students are interested, let them write short skits and use their masks in these plays. You can be certain that many children will want to make more paper bag masks for their make believe games at home!

CYLINDER MASKS

Materials needed: 12 × 18″ colored construction paper, stapler and staples or masking tape, colored paper and cloth scraps, scissors, and glue. (See Figure 8-3A.)

This activity provides practice in fine motor coordination, eye-hand coordination, translation, organization, generalization, and integration.

Present the challenge to your students of making a piece of paper stand right up and say, "Here I am!" "I'm sure that you each can think of someone special to you, some real or imaginary character that you enjoy," you begin. "Today we are going to make masks of those characters. We won't wear our personable masks. They will stand on their own!"

Use student ideas as energizers by asking how a 12 × 18″ piece of colored construction paper could be made to stand. "Surely, it

Figure 8-3A
Cylinder Masks

could be folded. But what would be the best way to suggest the roundness of a head? Yes! We can roll it into a cylinder!" Show the children how to join the 12" edges of the paper using staples or masking tape. White glue may also be used but is more difficult, especially for younger children, because the cylinder shape must be held in place until the glue dries. "Now, let's not leave the paper just standing around! Who are those characters you thought of ?" Answers are likely to include characters from cartoons, the community, the circus, or even the children's families!

Reach every individual by demonstrating ways to fashion the features of their favorite characters. Show the class how a nose or a beak may be made by folding a square of paper from corner to corner. Next, two adjacent edges are folded forward a fraction of an inch. These become tabs to attach the nose to the cylinder. (See Figure 8-3B.) Eyes are most effective if two colors of construction paper are used—one for the "white" of the eyes, the other for the pupils. Eyelashes and thin or bushy eyebrows complement the eyes. Mouths may be large or small, open or closed. A big smile can reveal pointy vampire teeth, a bunny's buck teeth, or the shiny square

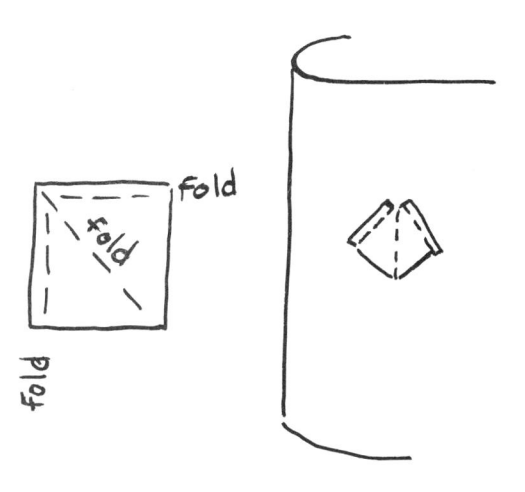

Figure 8-3B
Cylinder Masks

teeth of a star of stage and screen. Even a tongue might protrude in a pout! Strips of paper curled around a finger or pencil become hair. Or you may use yarn. Large pieces of paper may be cut and folded into hats. A half circle shaped into a cone is a good clown's hat. A whole circle cut along the radius may be formed into an oriental type hat or the brim of a sun hat. A hat can be drawn, cut out, and glued to the top front of the cylinder or stuck in two slots cut in the top edge.

Appreciate each person by providing mask making materials. Choose a child to pass out the 12 × 18" paper. Have the students take turns selecting paper scraps to get started. And give each a strip of masking tape about 8" long to stick the sides of the cylinder together. You may have students circulate a stapler if you prefer. You should circulate, too, sharing the fun.

Cylinder masks are a success if most children are indeed able to interpret a character that stands and says, "Here I am!" Line the masks up on your window sill to greet passers-by. Or use storybook people as subjects and have them parade along the shelves of your school library.

PRIMITIVE MASKS OF PAPIER-MÂCHÉ

Materials needed: aluminum foil, newspaper, wheat paste, containers, water, tempera paints, and brushes. Pictures of

Figure 8-4
Primitive Papier-Mâché Masks

primitive masks (American Indian, Eskimo, or African) are helpful, too. (See Figure 8-4.)

This activity provides practice in fine motor coordination, eye-hand coordination, auditory decoding, association, translation, organization, generalization, and integration.

Present the challenge to your class of gaining insight into and an appreciation of primitive cultures through mask making. To some people, masks are an important part of life. They have been and still are used for healing rituals and religious ceremonies. The Eskimos, for example, believed that animals had spirits which controlled them. The Eskimos depended upon animals for food, light, and clothing. Therefore, they honored animal spirits by making masks of them. These masks appeared to be part animal, part man. Eskimos hoped that the spirits, pleased with the masks, would continue to send the animals which they needed to survive.

Use student ideas as energizers as your class learns more about the Eskimo, his religion, and masks by asking what animals would be interpreted in Eskimo masks. Older groups, particularly, will realize that polar bears, seals, and a few birds,

Mask Making Magic 143

whales, walrus, and fish were necessary to the Eskimo. Skins were turned into warm clothing, meat was eaten, and fat or oil was used for lamps. "Eskimos had medicine men called 'Shamen' who wore masks when healing the sick. These masks were very frightening in order to scare away the evil spirits that caused illness. Eskimos also held contests to see who could make the funniest mask." Show the class photos of such masks if possible. The American Indian and some African tribes had similar beliefs and rituals. You may prefer to use either of these as an example, especially if it relates to geography or social studies units which you are discussing.

Reach every individual by explaining that papier-mâché will be used to make the masks, since it is quite durable and can be brightly painted. If your students are unfamiliar with this material, briefly describe that it consists of strips of newspaper dipped in wallpaper paste, and that it dries almost as hard as wood. Point out that it must be shaped over a base, in this case aluminum foil. Give each student a piece of foil about a foot long. The edges of the foil should be folded over so that the sheet is the size and shape of the student's face. Have the children press the foil against their faces, smoothing over the contours of forehead, nose, cheeks, and chin. The result will be an impression of each individual's face, and this will be the base for the papier-mâché primitive mask.

Appreciate each person as desks are covered with newspaper and grouped for sharing. Provide a container of wheat paste for each group—large cans from the hot lunch program are good. Cut the newspapers into strips a couple of inches wide and 3 or 4 inches long and put a pile of them in the center of each work area. Show your students how to dip them, one at a time, into the paste, removing the excess on the edge of the can or between thumb and forefinger. The foil base should be covered with a layer of this papier-mâché, carefully smoothed to remove wrinkles and then put to dry. By the next week every child should have a good idea of which characteristics of man and animal he wishes to combine in his mask, as details will be added in another session with paste and newspaper. Some of the features might include noses or beaks, horns, ears, prominent mouths, or protruding eyes. Observe that primitive artists often exaggerate important features. You may find that another look at photos of primitive art is helpful at this point. Instructions for adding details are found in

Chapter 4, lesson 2, Papier-Mâché Character Heads, along with suggestions for painting the completed project. Some students might enjoy using feathers, fur, or hair in finishing the masks.

Primitive masks from papier-mâché are a success if the children gain an understanding of beliefs and customs very different from theirs. The masks may be hung on your bulletin board with twine and tacks. Although silent, they will say a lot about learning in a very dramatic way. Each student might like to write a paragraph about which spirits are honored in his mask.

CIRCUS MASKS: PAPIER-MÂCHÉ OVER BIG BALLOONS

Materials needed: huge balloons, wheat paste, newspaper, containers, water, tempera paints, and brushes. A balloon pump might be appreciated, too! (See Figure 8-5.)

This activity provides practice in fine motor coordination, eye-hand coordination, auditory decoding, translation, organization, generalization, and integration.

Figure 8-5
Huge Circus Masks

Mask Making Magic 145

Present the challenge to your children of turning the classroom into a circus. Explain that big masks are needed because many circus creatures are very large. Explain that papier-mâché will be used to make the giant masks. Huge balloons will serve as bases for this project. The masks will indeed be very large and cover the whole head.

Use student ideas as energizers as each child chooses one creature that he finds especially appealing to make into a mask. Possibilities abound! There are clowns and acrobats, musicians and trapeze artists, lions and elephants, ponies and performing seals. And don't forget the ringmaster!

Reach every individual with a big balloon! They should be stretched in every direction to make blowing them up easier. A balloon pump, if you can get one, will make this step easier. This is an ambitious project, appropriate for older elementary students with previous experience with papier-mâché. Younger children could make two or three masks in a group effort. Cut newspapers into strips 3 to 4 inches wide using the paper cutter. Push the desks in your room together in sets of four or six. Put newspaper strips and a container of wheat paste in the center of each group, after covering all desks with newspaper. Strips moistened in the wheat paste are smoothed over each balloon leaving an opening at the bottom of the mask. The mask must fit over the head!

Appreciate each person after the first layer of papier-mâché has dried and hardened. The second step is a lot of fun! Long noses and large floppy ears for the elephant must be added. And the clowns should have cone shaped hats and bulbous noses! Round ears and nose will do for the lion. His mane could be of yarn, or maybe even a mop dyed yellow! Paper towel tubes and other cardboard shapes may be attached with masking tape and covered with the papier-mâché for some features. Others may be made according to the suggestions in Chapter 4, lesson 2, Papier-Mâché Character Heads. Patience, as well as imagination, is required as work must again dry before painting can be done. Large brushes should be used initially in the last step. Generally, you will observe that the more simple the paint job, the more striking the effect. Although students should be conservative with the paint, they can approach the final touches with abandon! How about real neckties around the necks of the masks or discarded and battered hats on their heads! Encourage everyone to add an amusing and unconventional accessory. All sorts of things are appropriate under the big top!

Huge papier-mâché circus masks are a success if students add patience to imagination and complete the splendid, oversized masks. Students can share their fun by having a circus parade through the school. Capes, blankets, or coats are good cover-ups to complete costumes. The masks can be an energizer for your language program. Have students write stories about the circus and act them out. A good time is had by all when the circus comes to town!

COLLAGE VISAGES: FACES WITH FEELING

Materials needed: 12 × 18″ colored construction paper, white glue, cloth and paper scraps, bottle caps, buttons, egg cartons, old magazines, other interesting odds and ends, and scissors. (See Figure 8-6.)

Figure 8-6
Collage Visage

This activity provides practice in fine motor coordination, eye-hand coordination, auditory decoding, sequencing, associa-

Mask Making Magic

tion, translation, organization, generalization, and integration.

Present the challenge of making a mask which shows feeling a day or so before you intend to do the project. Explain to the students that the masks will be collages and that they will need time to collect appropriate materials. Explain that collage means a picture or design made from many materials and pasted together. If possible, show the class some pictures of collage art, or better yet, an actual collage.

Use student ideas as energizers while you talk about the materials which are to be combined with imagination in a collage. Ask what are some unusual things which might be used as part of our collage masks. Buttons would make bright, happy eyes and bottle caps might be effective, too. Two sections of an egg carton, inverted and glued down, could be eyes popping with surprise or if painted, be plump and proud, puffy cheeks. Pipe cleaners may be twisted into frames for glasses or bent into a wry grin. Jar rubbers could be a big round mouth or wide open eyes. "You keep your eyes open, too," you encourage the children. "See how many interesting and appropriate things you can find."

Reach every individual with a discussion of feelings after the materials have been collected. Each should have in mind an emotion or feeling. Ask how one would feel if his little brother broke his new truck, or if he had bought an ice cream cone with his only quarter and dropped it, or if a mouse suddenly darted across the floor. Have the students demonstrate the facial features which would accompany the feelings described. Exaggeration helps!

Appreciate each person as the children make their emotional masks. You have provided paper for the background, cloth and paper scraps, and old magazines as supplements to each child's assortment. Suggest that a large paper scrap or a magazine page might be good for cutting out the shape of the face. Encourage the students to experiment with several effects before using the glue. Some may want to exchange some of their materials with other children. When a particular collage shows a lot of imagination, use it as an energizer by sharing it with the class. Children are good at making faces!

Collage masks of emotion are a success if each student portrays feeling in his work. Collecting unusual materials for an art project is a good stimulator. Most children are eager to discuss their feelings when given a chance, too. Before you display the masks, have each child give his a one sentence title such as "Fear is not fun" or "I was happy when I caught the fish," or have paragraphs composed about the masks.

Chapter 9

Discovering Whole New Worlds

HUGE CUT PAPER ANIMALS

Materials needed: 12 × 18" and 18 × 24" colored construction paper, colored paper scraps, scissors, and white glue. (See Figure 9-1.)

This activity provides practice in fine motor coordination, eye-hand coordination, auditory decoding, translation, organization, generalization, and integration.

Present the challenge to your students of stretching paper and their imaginations to create larger-than-life animals. "Most of us have animals that we especially like," you begin. "They may be pets that we have or wish we had, or they might be animals which we enjoy seeing at the zoo or in books. Because they are all so special, it might be fun to make some special pictures of them today."

Use student ideas as energizers in a discussion designed to help everyone think of as many different animals as possible. You

Figure 9-1

will find that individual ideas range from the pet cat at home who is a favorite because he follows his mistress everywhere, to the tiger at the zoo who is special because of his beautiful stripes; from the gerbil in a cage in the classroom who is soft and furry, to the giant panda in a picture book who looks like a huge toy.

Reach every individual as you explain and demonstrate how each child can put together his big cut paper pet. Choose any animal you wish as an example. A yellow cat might be good. Start with 12 × 18″ and 18 × 24″ yellow paper. You may prefer to use smaller sheets with very young groups. "The biggest part of the cat should be cut from the biggest piece of paper, shouldn't it?" you begin. "If I cut the corners from this 18 × 24″ rectangle, I will have a shape similar to that of a cat's body." Fringe the edges of the paper or cut it in an irregular curving line to make it look fluffy. The 12 × 18″ paper will be just right for the head! Again the corners are cut from the rectangle, achieving the appropriate shape while still leaving the paper as large as possible. This is glued to the body. The legs, tail, ears, and little details which make a pet special are cut from paper scraps and added.

Appreciate each person by organizing the class so that everyone may get the needed materials without unnecessary confusion. A few at a time may select their paper while you and a stu-

Discovering Whole New Worlds 151

dent helper or two pass out the glue and scissors. Urge the children to avoid copying you. A roomful of cats wouldn't be much fun! Some will want to know if they can add long necks for animals like giraffes, or cut the body thinner for a dachshund or even a snake. Emphasize that you showed them but one method and encourage creative thinking. For example, the large paper can be cut in two the long way, then pieced together to make it twice as long. That is a good way to make a long, thin animal!

Huge cut paper animals are a success if making something big seems to be a good energizer and using imagination in creating creatures as large as life was fun. This would be a good project to display on the walls in the hall outside your classroom. It will be a credit to the creativity inside!

SHAPES AS STARTERS

Materials needed: 8 × 12" colored construction paper, 12 × 18" manila paper, scissors, paste, and crayons. (See Figure 9-2.)

This activity provides practice in fine motor coordination, eye-hand coordination, association, translation, organization, generalization, and integration.

Figure 9-2

Present the challenge to children of letting the shape of a colored paper suggest the subject for an imaginative picture. Talking as you work, take a piece of 8 × 12" construction paper and cut from it a free-form shape. Explain that some shapes have names such as square, circle, or rectangle. "This shape that I am cutting is called a free-form shape because it is just a 'shape' shape. Free-form shapes can be bumpy or smooth, pointy or curved." Pass each child a piece of colored construction paper and have him cut a free-form shape. Collect them all.

Use student ideas as energizers as you hold up a few of the collected shapes for all to see and discuss. Ask students what the shapes suggest. Point out that each one looks a little different to each child.

Reach every individual by passing each a shape to use as a starter for his picture. "Look at the shape that you have been given and see what it looks like to you! Of course, you may have to add details with crayon to make it look more like what you have in mind. It is all right to swap with a friend if you see some possibilities in his paper scrap and he'd rather have yours." Pass out the paste and manila paper. Explain that the scrap should be pasted in the proper place on the manila paper and the necessary details added to it with a dark crayon. Then the entire picture should be brightly crayoned in.

Appreciate each person as imaginations go to work. If some child reaches a stalemate with his shape, hold it up for more student suggestions. Another child may want two identical shapes as starters. The first shape may be traced directly on the background or on colored construction paper and cut out. Two funny shapes are twice as amusing as one! A shape could be attached with a paper spring to give the work a three-dimensional effect. While direction following is surely desirable, so is creative thinking and problem solving.

Shapes as starters is a success if many unusual subjects for pictures are suggested. Have students title their pictures and display them where the many ideas can be enjoyed. Use them as energizers for a creative writing class by having children write paragraphs about their pictures.

WHAT COMES FROM AN EGG?

Materials needed: 12 × 18" manila paper, crayons, watercolor paints, water, and brushes. (See Figure 9-3.)

Discovering Whole New Worlds 153

Figure 9-3

This activity provides practice in fine motor coordination, eye-hand coordination, translation, organization, generalization, and integration.

Present the challenge to your class of using their imaginations, crayons, and paint to make an "X-ray" picture of an egg that contains a surprise. Point out that birds, snakes, and many types of fish all get their start in an egg. In most cases, we know what will hatch from an egg by its size and shape. "Today we are going to make pictures of some unusual eggs. We will draw them in cross section so that we can see inside, and what is inside will be amazing!"

Use student ideas as energizers by asking, "What are some things that you would never, ever expect to find in an egg? Sure, a brown dog, an old shoe, or an elephant would certainly be surprises! What else can you think of?" Explain that almost anything put inside an egg would have to be bent into an oval!

Reach every individual as you describe how the X-ray drawings should be done. The egg shape should be almost as large as your paper so that there will be a cross section view. That is, we will pretend that the front of the egg has been cut away so that only the shape of the egg remains and we can see what is inside. Remember that the creature or object inside the egg must fit there snugly. Therefore, you will have to show how they are bent or curled to conform to the contour of an egg. Some things don't bend or curl easily. These could be distorted or changed to make them the right shape. After all, a car doesn't really come from an egg, so the car in the egg needn't look real!

Appreciate each person as the drawings are developed. Each egg has a surprise for you! You will observe that the shape of an egg is a good energizer in encouraging unusual drawings. The fantasy and fun of the activity is especially helpful to your students who tend to be somewhat self-conscious or inhibited in their art work. The final step will be a watercolor wash. The crayon work must be heavy enough to show through the paint.

"What comes from an egg?" is a successful subject for pictures if children respond well to the amusing though absurd notion that anything can be hatched. Students add a watercolor wash of a complementary color over the area inside the egg and you display them around your classroom. They will arouse much curiosity and comment!

A DISTANT PLANET

Materials needed: crayons, markers, pastels, and 12 × 18" manila paper. (See Figure 9-4.)

This activity provides practice in fine motor coordination, eye-hand coordination, auditory decoding, translation, generalization, and integration.

Present the challenge to your space age students of combining fact and fantasy in order to picture life on another planet. "Not too many years ago, before the days of satellites and lunar launchings, people wondered if there might be civilizations on some other planet," you begin. "Today we are learning more each day about our solar system. We even have pieces of the moon and pictures of its landscape. Still, it is fun to speculate whether life exists elsewhere in the universe and to try and imagine what the inhabitants of another planet and environment might be like."

Use student ideas as energizers while you make your own imaginary space exploration. "The inhabitants on another planet might look a great deal like us," you continue, "or very different. No matter what their appearance, they would have to solve many of the same problems we are trying to solve in

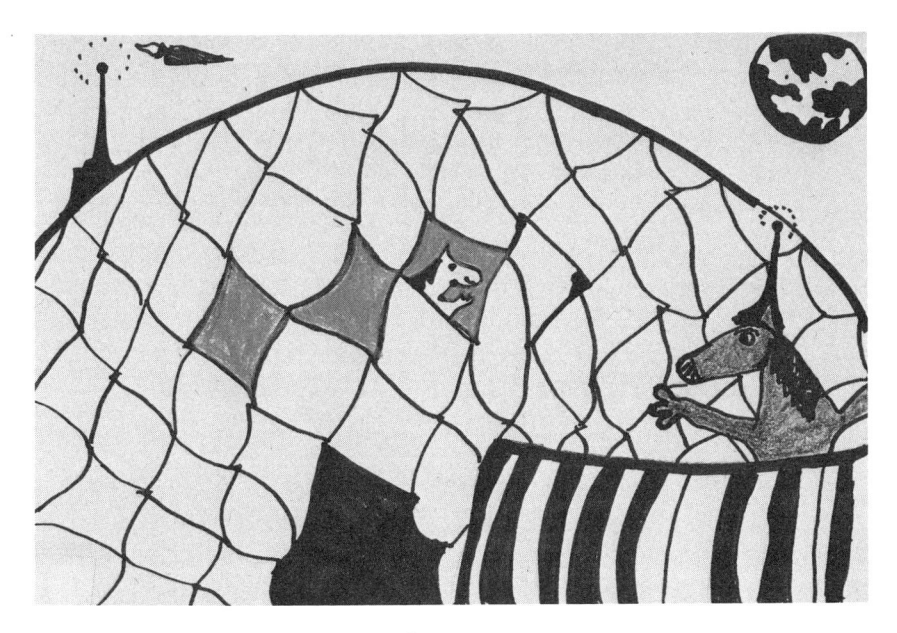

Figure 9-4

order to live together. What might these be? Yes! They would need food, of course. Perhaps there would be trees with apples as big as pumpkins or gardens of bright pink lettuce and rose-like flowers that are delicious in salads, or maybe they would get their food from machines which dispense whole dinners in wafer form."

Reach every individual as you continue the discussion which helps children to visualize the pictures that they will be drawing and also develops an awareness of problems that must be solved in any society. "What is another necessity besides food?" you continue. "Surely there must be shelter! How houses look would depend upon the climate and available building materials," you point out. "Bright tents or canopies would do in a warm climate. One might find stone houses on a rocky terrain. In a land with many lakes, homes might be boats or built on wharfs. Or perhaps the people have discovered fantastic building materials that enable them to build homes with incredible shapes that look like sculpture or that are transparent and heated by the sun or that are even mysteriously suspended in midair!"

Appreciate each person by taking the time to let your students share their ideas. Transportation and clothes must be considered, too. When you are sure that the subject of space has been thoroughly explored and everyone seems anxious to put the mental pictures developed during discussion on paper, pass out the drawing materials. Each child should select one topic—either food, shelter, transportation, or clothing—to picture. Drawing should be done with black crayons or markers and brightly colored in with crayons or pastels.

Drawing life on a distant planet is a success if the children understand that the speculation is only fantasy and brings freedom and fun to their art work. You will also find that considering the problems of any civilization is a good energizer for social studies. The pictures are a bright and colorful reflection of a flight from earth on a spacecraft called imagination!

ABSURD MONTAGES

Materials needed: old magazines, 12 × 18" colored construction paper, colored paper scraps, crayons, scissors, and glue. (See Figure 9-5.)

This activity provides practice in fine motor coordination, eye-hand coordination, auditory decoding, translation, organization, generalization, and integration.

Present the challenge to children of combining ordinary photos in an extraordinary way to present a picture of something that could never happen. "These old magazines are full of attractive pictures of life as we know it. It might be fun to cut some of them out and use our imaginations as we put them together in an amusing or amazing way," you suggest. "For example, we might make a woman wearing a pie for a hat or someone sitting smack in the middle of an ice cream sundae! When parts of photos are mounted together on a background, it is called montage," you explain.

Use student ideas as energizers as they look at the magazines. Give them scissors so that they may cut out pictures as they thumb through the pages. While they work, pass out the 12 × 18" construction paper so that they can begin to arrange their compositions. Stimulate the slower starting students by using other children's efforts as examples. Seeing how others are solving the problem will help them to approach the project, too. Did you ever see a car on the kitchen ceiling?

Reach every individual with your interest in each child's work. Some of them are pretty silly, to be sure! That's the point of

Figure 9-5

this project, so enjoy it along with the children. When most of the class is finished with the magazines, have them arrange the parts of their montage on the background paper. It is still too early to paste them in place, however.

Appreciate each person by helping individuals evaluate their work. Give suggestions as needed. In some cases, a part of a magazine picture may be used as a pattern in order to cut an identical shape from construction paper. Repeating shapes can be part of good composition. Or some of the parts of the montage can be outlined to accent their shape. Other figures can be drawn in with crayon, if that would help to better express the child's idea. Overlapping helps, too. When each student is satisfied with his arrangement, have him glue the parts in place and title his work.

Absurd montages are a success if everyone achieves a silly assemblage. This activity is a good one for students who lack

158   Imagination and Environment as Energizers

confidence in their ability. They are able to solve the problem without drawing, yet get some practice in recognizing the elements of good composition such as shape, color, balance, and unity. It might be fun to write stories about the nonsense notions!

CLOTH AND CRAYON CREATURES

Materials needed: 12 × 18″ colored construction paper, crayons, colorful cloth scraps, scissors, and glue. (See Figure 9-6.)

Figure 9-6

This activity provides practice in fine motor coordination, eye-hand coordination, auditory decoding, translation, organization, generalization, and integration.

Present the challenge to children of using cloth and crayons to create a collection of animals that would never be seen in a zoo. "Mother nature has given many animals handsome and colorful patterns. Some of these patterns, like the spots on a speckled trout, are designed to help the creature hide in his environment," you explain. "Others, like that on the peacock's magnificent tail, only make him more bright and beautiful. There are patterns on these cloth scraps, too. They don't look like the patterns found in nature," you continue, "but it might be fun to imagine what sort of creatures might bear such interesting markings."

Use student ideas as energizers as you examine some of the scraps and ask students what animal they might belong to. A pattern of yellow flowers could be a cow who grazes among yellow daisies each day, or it might be the fur of a 'dandy' lion! Stripes would be excellent for a zebra-like animal; calico is perfect for the calico cat we have all heard of but never seen.

Reach every individual by giving directions which will help put his ideas on paper. "First we will take turns choosing a scrap of cloth from this assortment," you begin. "Next we will decide what sort of animal the pattern of the material suggests to us. The cloth must then be cut into the proper shape for that animal's body. Head, legs, and tail can also be cut from the cloth or added with crayon after the cloth is glued to the background paper. Finally, we will tell more about the animal that we have created by using our crayons to draw his habitat.

Appreciate each person by giving individual attention after students have selected their scraps and the 12 × 18" colored construction paper has been passed out. You may discover that some students have difficulty cutting the cloth. Folding the cloth over the lower blade of the scissors and pulling down while pulling up with the scissors may help. The cloth can also be torn. Or several scraps may be pieced together to get the desired shape. The background should be colored bright in order to show up as well as its colorful cloth inhabitant! Some work may be made more attractive if the body of the animal and other important parts of the picture are outlined with a dark crayon.

Cloth and crayon animals are a success if each is unique and students enjoy using their imaginations in drawing the details of their creature's environment. Have each student write a sentence on the picture surface describing his animal. Or expand the sentences into paragraphs for your next language lesson.

INVENTIONS THAT SHOULD BE INVENTED

Materials needed: 12 × 18" colored construction paper or manila drawing paper, crayons, white glue, and assorted scraps such as string, yarn, cloth, toothpicks, Popsicle sticks, pipe cleaners, and bits of styrofoam or cardboard. (See Figure 9-7.)

This activity provides practice in fine motor coordination, eye-hand coordination, auditory decoding, translation, organization, generalization, and integration.

Present the challenge of becoming inventors to the children in your class, then have them make two-dimensional models of their inventions. "Many things have been invented to help people accomplish more easily work that must be done. Tractors plow gardens, huge street sweepers clean the streets, toasters make our breakfast toast, and machines wash our clothes," you point out. "Yet there are lots of jobs that still must be done by hand. Today we are going to invent some machines to help us with such chores, both big and small."

Use student ideas as energizers as your students think of types of work that might be better done by machine. Ask what some of those tasks are and what sort of contraption could do them for us. For example, a garbage-taker-outer could run on a track from the kitchen to the trash cans outside. A baby sitting machine could perhaps be sort of a computer, programmed to protect the baby from danger and keep him out of

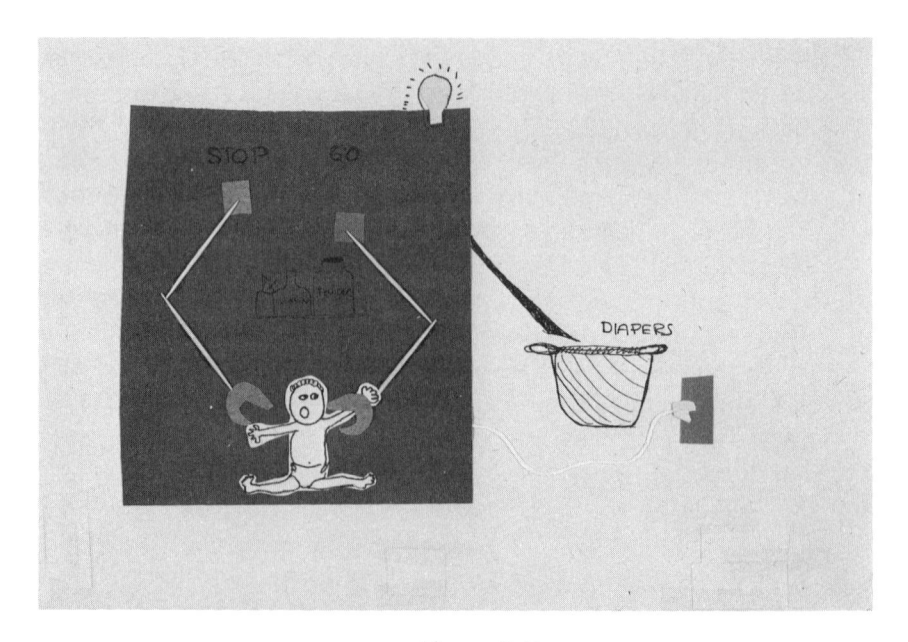

Figure 9-7

Discovering Whole New Worlds   161

mischief. It might have an arm-like diaper changing device on the side and include some baby feeding equipment!

Reach every individual with directions when everyone understands the problem and is on the way to solving it with an idea of his own. "This 12 × 18" paper will be the background to draw your discoveries on. Every machine has moving parts in order to do its job," you point out. "These parts can be made from some of the scraps I have here. There is cardboard or styrofoam from which to cut wheels or pulleys, and there are toothpicks and Popsicle sticks, as well as other odds and ends.

Appreciate each person by noticing which children seem slow in starting. If lack of ideas is the problem, ask what chore the child dislikes most. Help him to use his imagination to visualize what sort of machine might be able to do the job for him. When all the inventors are involved in their work, you know that they have accepted the challenge.

Inventions that should be invented are a success if each young Edison comes up with some sort of contraption. The pictures of the inventions can be completed by adding a drawing of the inventor or another person using the machine, and each contraption can be titled. You will want to display the work, for the children will be anxious to see how their classmates tackled jobs that had to be done.

CRAYON AND FINGER PAINT: UNDERSEA EXCURSIONS

Materials needed: finger paint paper cut to 12 × 18" (older groups might enjoy working larger), crayons, water, blue finger paint, towels, and newspapers to cover the desks. (See Figure 9-8.)

This activity provides practice in fine motor coordination, eye-hand coordination, translation, organization, generalization, and integration.

Present the challenge to your class of combining crayons and finger paints to make pictures of worlds hidden far beneath the sea. Explain that, far out to sea, the floor of the ocean is something of a mystery to us. Through science we are increasing our knowledge, but still we can only guess at many marvelous sights which remain hidden from our eyes.

Figure 9-8

Use student ideas as energizers as you make an imaginary descent to the ocean floor. "We have learned from books that we are sure to find some things like coral reefs and crayfish. Let's imagine some surprises, too," you suggest. Fact and fantasy mingle in the replies which could include electric eels of vibrant colors, giant and dangerous squid, streamlined skates which speed along, and incredible rock formations which have been sculpted by the sea, as well as mermaids with hair floating behind them, sunken ships with stores of treasure spilling onto the sand, and mysterious cities built before history began and crumbling now under the shifting undersea currents.

Reach every individual by giving each a chance to create his concept of the ocean floor on paper. Explain that the drawing will be done with crayon on finger paint paper. Students must be sure to use the shiny, smooth side. Emphasize that the crayon work must be as thick and bright as possible because finger paints are to be rubbed over it. The wax of the crayons must be heavy enough to repel the water and paint. When the pictures are complete, it is time to finger paint on the final touches.

Appreciate each person by supervising every child carefully during the painting process. Too much paint could ruin the picture.

Discovering Whole New Worlds

You can have each child cover his desk with newspaper, or you may prefer to have individuals take turns using the paints at one work station. Demonstrate how a quarter cup of water is poured at the center of the paper. This is then smoothed over the paper and out to the edges. A generous tablespoon of blue finger paint is placed in the center of the picture and rubbed over the paper. When it is smooth and free of lumps and splotches, the finger painting may be done. Make seaweed with a finger or with the side of an open hand in a wavy, upward motion. Snails may be made with the soft side of a fist in a curling movement. Circular sea creatures are suggested by placing the side of an open hand on the paper and rotating it. Can students think of other techniques? Of course! Experiments are fine. Mistakes can be smoothed away easily.

Crayon and finger paint seascapes are a success if each picture portrays an imaginary descent into the sea. Finger painting is always a student favorite and working first with crayon enables individuals to express their ideas clearly. Don't stop here! Make the most of a good energizer as students write stories about adventures on the ocean floor!

Chapter 10

Individualized Awareness Activities

CUT PAPER FISH

Materials needed: 12 × 18" colored construction paper, paper scraps, scissors, paste. (See Figure 10-1.)

This activity provides practice in translation, organization, fine motor coordination, eye-hand coordination, and generalization.

Present the challenge by asking what are some of the things which we know about fish. Encourage individuals to think by asking how are fish shaped. Why? How and what do they breath? How do they move? What is the texture of their skin? Invite your children to sit on the floor by the aquarium in your room. If there is none, visit one elsewhere in the school if possible. Discuss the students' observations. Notice how fish are colored to blend with undersea life where they live; observe how they are designed to obtain the particular food they eat.

Figure 10-1

Use student ideas as energizers while you demonstrate the approach to the project. "The large paper is to be the fish," you begin. "What shape shall I cut? Sure! A long oval will do for a fat fish. We will use scraps for details. What are some of the important parts? Yes, mouth, eyes, gills, fins, and a tail! Circles or half circles become scales. We can cut more than one at a time by folding the paper."

Reach every individual by noting which did not participate in the discussion. After the children have materials and are going to work, move about the room and speak with the quieter children. Give them a chance to tell you their ideas. Notice if a child needs help cutting the basic shape. Some children may require another look at the aquarium; some may need reminding that the scraps which contrast to the scales make brighter eyes, tails, and other details.

Appreciate each person by showing how one has noticed something unique, how another is approaching the project in an unusual way, how still another is making a remarkable fish. This further stimulates and encourages an individual approach. When the project is complete, display the fish. Sometime take a break from routine and talk about what is special about each person's fish.

Individualized Awareness Activities

Cut paper fish are successful if each child participates and most of the fish, although not entirely biologically accurate, are unique. Younger children might enjoy making an experience chart about what they learned; older children could write a paragraph themselves. If they retain many points of the discussion, your lesson has succeeded.

SELF-PORTRAITS

Materials needed: 12 × 18" manila paper, water paints or tempera paints, brushes, water containers, paper towels, newspapers to cover desks.

This activity provides practice in fine motor coordination, integration, and generalization.

Present the challenge by asking if anyone knows what a self-portrait is. Once it is established that a self-portrait is a picture of the artist by the artist, it would help to look at some together. Several good examples should be available in books at your school or community library.

Use student ideas as energizers as you look at these reproductions together. Ask if the self-portraits look like photos. Was the artist painting how he looked or how he felt? Why did he use so much of a certain color? Why do you think that he wanted to paint this picture since we have photos of him? These questions obviously don't have right or wrong answers. They are intended only to stimulate your students to think about and respond to the art work as individuals.

Reach every individual as you help students think about painting their own self-portraits. Begin by asking, "What shape is your head. Try putting one hand on top of your head, the other under your chin. How does it feel? Now, what about the shape of your head? Of course! Almost like an egg! There is something special about each of us," you point out. "What is special about you?" Have a mirror available so that each child can take a good look at himself before he begins, and can refer back to it if he needs to as he works.

Appreciate each person by walking around the room and encouraging individuals as they work. All will have something special about their paintings, just as there is something special about them. Suggest that they use their favorite color in the background or add a favorite toy. Ask them if they would like to try cut paper or crayon self-portraits in their spare time.

They may be pleased with the results and want to put the work up with the others. The contrast of a different media would have an interesting effect in the display.

Self-portraits are a success if most of the children complete the activity with pleasure. Follow up the exercise by having the children write a paragraph on "I am special because . . ." First graders could write several sentences: My name is _____. I have _____ eyes and _____ hair. I like to _____." It can be fun for parents to find their child's portrait mounted on the back of his chair when they come to school for PTA or open house.

PATTERNS FOUND IN NATURE

Materials needed: 12 × 18" colored construction paper, paper scraps, paste, and scissors. (See Figure 10-2.)

This activity provides practice in translation, organization, eye-hand coordination, and fine motor coordination.

Present the challenge by asking if the children have noticed how nature has especially designed creatures to fit their surroundings—even the season of the year.

Use student ideas as energizers as you think together of as many examples as possible. The tawny leopard has spots which make him difficult to see in the jungle where he lives. Tropical birds are brightly colored like the lush foliage of their habitat. Giraffes and zebras are among the unusual and beautiful creatures the children are likely to think of. Closer to home, striped bass and spotted salmon are hard to see in shimmery lakes and rivers. Explain to students that repeated markings like this are called patterns.

Reach every individual in your class by being aware that some may not have had the experience through zoo trips, living close to nature, or books to readily understand the concept. Have available photos of some typical examples to help these individuals conceptualize the idea. Allow each child to select a piece of construction paper from which to cut the shape of the animal he wishes to make, and have scraps for the stripes or spots of the pattern. Help to ensure a variety of creatures from the air, water, and land by reviewing the possibilities previously discussed as children get their materials.

Individualized Awareness Activities 169

Figure 10-2

Appreciate each person through your enthusiasm at the progress as children begin to use paste and scissors. One child may be making a creature nobody thought of. Another may be using red or orange paper for a tiger. "That's fine, for we know that an artist is not a camera!" Point these unusual approaches out to "energize" the other artists. Some children will cut the animal shape all in one piece; some may find it easier to do one section at a time.

Patterns in nature are a success if each animal pictured bears a pattern, and the children are eager to display the pictures! Why not invite other classes to visit your cut paper "zoo"? Selected individuals could tell about the creature they made, where it lives, what it eats, and its habits. The activity can be integrated into a language lesson if the children write stories about their patterned creatures.

CENTER DESIGNS IN NATURE

Materials needed: 12 × 18" colored construction paper, crayons, pastels or chalk, an apple, orange, pepper, onion, daisy, vegetables, or flowers. (See Figure 10-3.)

This activity provides practice in fine motor coordination, eye-hand coordination, translation, and organization.

Figure 10-3

Present the challenge by asking children if they have noticed what interesting designs are to be found, sometimes hidden, at the center of growing things. Hold up an apple and ask what will be discovered if the apple is cut in two. Dissect the apple across the core and a star-shaped design appears in cross section. "What about an orange?" you continue. Dissect the orange also. Explain the terms "dissect" and "cross section."

Use student ideas as energizers as you discuss what the designs remind them of. Can they think of other designs found at the center of growing things that they have seen? What part of the plant or fruit is making this design at the center? "Right!" The seeds. They are protected by the fruit surrounding

Individualized Awareness Activities

them." Notice how often part of the design is made by a protective case for seeds, such as in the apple. This activity could be part of a study unit about seeds or some other science lesson involving plants.

Reach every individual by letting each child or group of children select one of the flowers or fruits to draw in cross section on the construction paper with the chalk or pastels. Suggest that they draw it much larger than life so that the design will really show up. Explain that they are going to be able to draw several things, so room should be left on the paper for three or four designs. Notice if some child has on a shirt or dress with a pattern suggesting a center design, or wear such an item yourself. Can your children see any other similar pattern on clothing in the room?

Appreciate each person by encouraging individuals as they work. If some child is having trouble, find out whether it is a "seeing" or "drawing" problem. Either can be solved if you help him simplify the shapes he sees by talking about them with him. As students complete the drawings, let them swap fruits or flowers with each other. Point out that overlapping their cross section drawings makes their pictures more attractive.

Drawing center designs from nature is a success if most of the children perceive the designs and translate them into a drawing. The new words "dissect" and "cross section" will increase vocabularies. Later children might like to select one center design to use in a potato print pattern. (See Part I, Chapter 3.)

HAPPY FACES

Materials needed: 12 × 18" colored construction paper, paper scraps, and paste. (See Figure 10-4.)

This activity will provide practice in organization, fine motor control, generalization, integration, and verbal endings.

Present the challenge by asking students what happens to their faces when they are really happy. What about the shape of their eyes? How does the mouth change? What are dimples? Does anything happen to noses? Why do people speak of a long face?

Use student ideas as energizers as you talk about some of the happenings that would make the children have a happy face. Many children will have ideas. Some individuals will enjoy

Figure 10-4

"energizing" their classmates by showing how they might look if mother surprised them with a new kitten or dad brought home tickets to the ball game.

Reach every individual by realizing that some children are not likely to receive surprises of toys, clothes, or other material things. Help them relate to the activity by including in the discussion "happy happenings" that don't depend on money. Why do people say that "the best things in life are free? Do you think it is true? Do the same things make all of us happy, or is each of us different?"

Appreciate each person as the children select materials and go to work. Suggest that each individual choose a "happy" color of construction paper from which to make the shape of the face. The face should be cut almost as large as the paper, so only cut away a little of the outside edge of the paper. Encourage the students to exaggerate the features just for fun. Move around the room as the children work. If some child has a particularly happy face in progress, motivate the other students by showing it to them and asking if they can tell why this face looks especially jolly.

Individualized Awareness Activities

Happy faces are a success if each individual selects a bright color for his face and exaggerates the features. The activity is also successful if most of the faces are different and reflect an individual approach to the project. Use the project as an energizer for having individuals draw about something that made them very happy, or have children draw about a time when they made someone else happy.

AQUARIUM WAX RESIST PICTURES

Materials needed: 12 × 18" manila paper, crayons, brushes, diluted blue tempera or watercolor paints, and newspaper to cover desks. (See Figure 10-5.)

Figure 10-5

This activity provides practice in auditory decoding, fine motor coordination, eye-hand coordination, generalization, integration, and organization.

Present the challenge by inviting the children to sit on the floor by the aquarium in your classroom. If there is none, arrange to visit one in another room of your school. Stimulate the children's thoughts by asking them why they think that this is a good place for the fish to live.

Use student ideas as energizers as they respond to the challenge. What do they notice that makes this aquarium a pleasant environment for fish? Do the pebbles at the bottom of the tank or the seaweeds serve a purpose? How does the tank compare with a lake, ocean, or stream?

Reach every individual by asking what children have observed about other aquariums they might have seen. Ask if any have aquariums at home and how their fish are cared for. Having them share their observations will provide enrichment for children lacking this background experience.

Appreciate each person by asking him what he would include in an aquarium if he had one. Explain that crayons will be used to draw a fish tank large enough to fill most of the 12 × 18" paper. The fish and details of their habitat are also to be drawn with crayons and colored in brightly. (The crayon resist process is explained in Chapter 2.) As they work, appreciate their efforts, noticing original ideas or special effects. Continue to use student ideas as energizers by showing outstanding examples to the class. Outstanding should not mean the best drawing. Ideally, the word should include use of an unusual color, well thought out content, or dramatic arrangement of the objects on the paper. Paint is brushed on last of all.

Aquarium pictures are a success if children understand the discussion and are able to approach their drawings confidently and eagerly. Use this lesson as an energizer for language arts by having students write on topics such as "Our aquarium" or "I like (or don't like) being a fish because" from the point of view of a fish.

PAINTING A PET

Materials needed: tempera or water color paints, large brushes, 12 × 18" manila paper, water containers, paper towels, and newspaper to cover desks. (See Figure 10-6.)

This activity provides practice in fine motor coordination, translation, generalization, and integration.

Individualized Awareness Activities

Figure 10-6

Present the challenge by bringing or having a student bring a suitable pet to the classroom. A hamster or gerbil would do fine, but a more unusual animal might function even more effectively—how unusual depends on your courage!

Use student ideas as energizers as you and your class take the time to appreciate the pet. Begin by asking what characteristics the children notice about the animal. Do these characteristics help him obtain or eat his food? What does the pet eat? How does his master care for him? Also discuss how this animal is different from other animals.

Reach every individual by inviting the children to pet the animal. Remind them not to hurt or scare the pet. Encourage children to tell about their own pets at home. This provides an excellent opportunity for the child who seldom participates in discussions. Your interest in his ideas will give him confidence.

Appreciate each person as the class begins to paint. (Hints for passing out materials and painting are found in Chapter 2.) Once again some youngsters may need help in simplifying some shapes they see. "Do you think the head is round? Could you paint the ears as triangles?" It is best not to meet the reluctant child "head on." Urge this child to participate by painting his favorite animal from memory.

Painting a pet is a success if each student makes a visual response to the experience. Have children write paragraphs about the

176 Imagination and Environment as Energizers

pet to be displayed with the paintings. An experience chart would better serve smaller students. Some might like to find a library book about that kind of animal. Ask if the children would like to do a crayon or pencil picture of their pets at home. This could provide a topic for sharing time another day.

DETAIL DRAWINGS OF THE ROOM

Materials needed: ball point pens, 12 × 18" manila paper or newsprint, and crayons for younger children. Pencils for older children could be substituted if necessary. (See Figure 10-7.)

This activity provides practice in fine motor coordination, eye-hand coordination, space perception, integration, and generalization.

Present the challenge by asking the children to close their eyes and put their heads on their desks. Ask them to recall some of the larger features of the room; ask them if they remember some of the details. "What are the walls made of? How many doors are there? What is in the back left corner? Now let's open our eyes!"

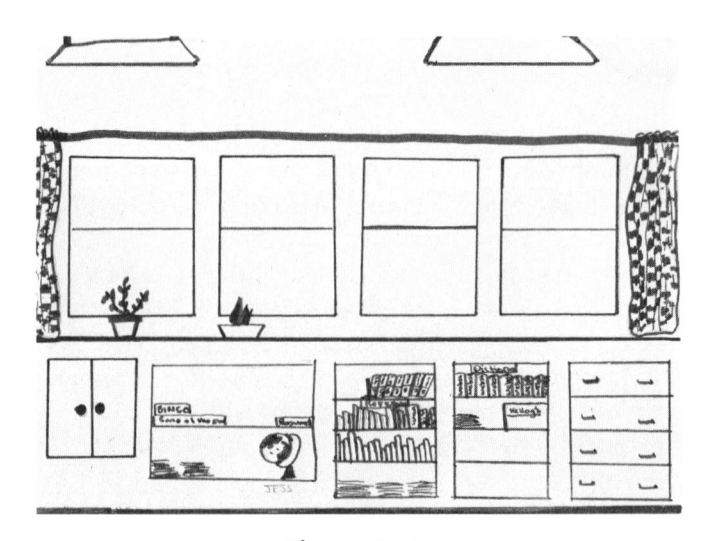

Figure 10-7

Use student ideas as energizers in becoming more aware of the surroundings. "What are some of the things we didn't remember with our eyes closed?" Explain that pens will be used

Individualized Awareness Activities 177

for drawing for three reasons: 1) they have a fine point and are good for drawing details; 2) pen and ink drawings are darker and show up better than pencil drawings; and 3) we won't be tempted to erase. Have each child select one wall to draw.

Reach every individual as the children begin drawing. You will quickly see which one hesitates. Help this child to generalize what he sees by asking what shapes he notices. Encourage the child who is easily frustrated by pointing out that he is an artist, not a camera. Nobody expects his drawing to be as precise as a photo. Show him how an incorrect line may be fixed by drawing over it without erasing. In any group there is likely to be a child who is confused and upset at the prospect of detail room drawing. Suggest that this child select one object to draw. Thus encouraged by a small success, he can try to draw more of the room in his spare time.

Appreciate each person by displaying his work. Notice if a particular child handled a certain drawing problem well. Call it to the attention of the others. This could provide, for example, a mini-lesson in perspective drawing.

Detail drawings of the room are a success if each person completes a drawing. Awareness increases if many of the details not remembered with eyes closed are included in the drawings. It becomes a real success experience when it is an energizer for doing similar drawings of rooms at home!

SCRAPWOOD SURPRISES

Materials needed: tempera paints, brushes, water, paper towels, newspapers to cover the desks, and a small scrapwood board for each child. Sources of wood are suggested in the first lesson of Chapter 4. (See Figure 10-8.)

This activity provides practice in fine motor coordination, eye-hand coordination, association, translation, organization, generalization, and integration.

Present the challenge to each child in your class of discovering a character held captive within a bit of scrapwood. "Have you ever noticed that many pieces of wood appear to have pictures on them?" you begin. "These pictures may be suggested by the grain of the wood or by knot holes and other ir-

Figure 10-8

regularities. Or it may be simply the shape of the scrap that reminds us of something or someone."

Use student ideas as energizers by pulling a few pieces of wood from the pile to study and discuss. A piece with two dark knot holes might suggest eyes glaring out like an angry lion or maybe a bear disturbed during his hibernation! A piece with a single knot hole and the lines of the wood grain curving around it could be a person in profile with a dark eye and large nose! Or the grain could suggest rolling hills or perhaps the ocean's swell. A landscape or seascape as well as a creature may be held captive in the wood!

Reach every individual with a chance to put his ideas down in paint. The room should be organized so that the sharing of materials is easy. Desks are covered with newspaper and pushed together in groups of four or six. In the center of each group are paints and paper towels. Each student has both a large and a small paint brush. Let the students select their wood and examine it carefully front and back and from all sides. Can everyone find a captive there, waiting to be released with a paint brush?

Appreciate each person by helping the child who has trouble seeing a "surprise" in his piece of wood. Help him reexamine it. "Don't paint over the part of the wood that suggested your picture," you advise another. "It is more fun if the knot hole

Individualized Awareness Activities

or wood grain that gave you your inspiration can be seen!" Add that it is best to develop only one idea on each board. Lots of detail in the background would be distracting. Black paint should be reserved for the final touches, then applied sparingly with a small brush.

Scrapwood surprises are a success if letting the wood itself suggest a subject for a picture really activated the young imaginations! After the paints have dried, brush a coat of shellac on each board to preserve the painting. Someone at home will be next to find a pleasant surprise!

Chapter 11

Mini-Excursions as Energizers

WONDERFUL WEEDS

Materials needed: 12 × 18" manila paper and ball point pens. (See Figure 11-1.)

This activity provides practice in fine motor coordination, eye-hand coordination, translation, generalization, and integration.

Present the challenge to your botanists of studying the intricacies of weeds both above and below the ground. Take your class outside along the edge of the playground. Point out that weeds are very interesting plants and that there are many different kinds. Some even have blossoms. Have each child pull up a weed carefully so that it comes up from the ground roots and all. The plant needs its roots for nourishment. Roots are interesting to look at, too.

Use student ideas as energizers once you have returned to the classroom. Hold up a few of the weeds, one at a time, for students to observe and discuss. "What are some of the de-

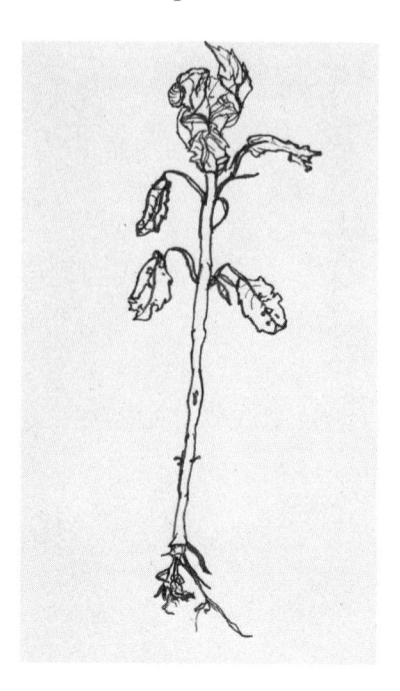

Figure 11-1

tails that we see on this plant?" you ask. Notice the shape of its leaves, if they have smooth or jagged edges, as well as the fine network of veins running from its stem to its tip. Discuss the roots with their crooked contours and tiny, hair-like fibrils. Blossoms should be mentioned, too, especially the varying shapes of their petals.

Reach every individual as you explain that each student is to pretend that he is looking at his weed through a microscope. "That means that we will be drawing our plant larger than life. In this way we can better include the many small but important details. We will work with pens since they have fine points which are good for drawing tiny parts like the veins or the fibrils. Pen and ink drawings are also darker and show up more than those done in pencil," you add. Pass out the paper and pens. "Try to stretch your drawings from the bottom to the top of your paper," you urge the class.

Appreciate each person by pointing out that careful observation is an extremely important part of drawing. Remind students to show the shapes of leaves and the veins, the contours of roots and the fibrils. You are likely to find that some child is worried about pen lines which cannot be erased. "If you make a

Mini-Excursions as Energizers

line that is wrong, simply change it to make it right and darken it. It will not be noticed when you are finished." Another youngster may have problems beginning his drawing. Have him do a sketch of just one leaf on the edge of his paper. If this is successful, he may be willing to try drawing several leaves on the stem and the roots. Students need not draw every single leaf; only enough to suggest the shape of the plant.

Drawing wonderful weeds in detail is a success if the children discover more both about plants and drawing at the same time. They learn that observation is essential to art and they find that the part of a plant usually hidden is interesting, too. If most of your students complete a drawing, you know that your encouragement is a good energizer.

SOUNDS WHILE SITTING STILL

Materials needed: 12 × 18" manila paper, dark markers, and pastels. (See Figure 11-2.)

Figure 11-2

This activity provides practice in fine motor coordination, eye-hand coordination, association, translation, and integration.

Present the challenge to your students of taking a very special field trip, appropriately enough, to a field! Have the children sit quietly for several minutes. This might be a challenge in itself! They should close their eyes and listen carefully, trying to identify as many sounds as possible—not just the loud, obvious ones. Soft sounds, often unnoticed, should be heard as well.

Use student ideas as energizers when you return to your classroom by asking what sounds were especially interesting. Responses may include a mother calling her toddler, a dog barking, the song of a bird, the buzz of a bug, and the wind in the trees. Or passing traffic, footsteps, the bell on a bike, and a motorcycle might be mentioned.

Reach every individual as you explain that each child should choose one sound that he found most interesting. He should imagine what was making the noise and how it looked. Dark markers will be used to draw pictures of the sources of the sounds. When the line drawings with markers are finished, color will be added with pastels.

Appreciate each person after the paper, markers, and pastels have been passed out and the children become absorbed. It is not unusual for a small artist to make the sound of a siren as he draws a firetruck. That's a sure sign that he has been energized! Some children may ask to sketch with a pencil before using their markers. This is a good temporary solution for the timid or particular child. Eventually, however, with your encouragement he should become confident enough to express his ideas directly with marker. Be sure that students add pastel to the background of their pictures to disguise any fingerprints made while working. The pastel may be used on its side for such broad areas of color.

Drawing sounds heard while sitting still is a success for all of your students if they are able to transform a sound into a scene. Why not have them describe the sound that they liked with words, too? A sentence saying what each heard and why he liked it could be mounted across the bottom of every picture when they are displayed. Or have your older students write paragraphs about sounds heard while sitting still.

LOOKING AT THE WIND

Materials needed: 12 × 18" manila paper, crayons, watercolor paints or diluted blue tempera paint, water, and brushes. (See Figure 11-3.)

Mini-Excursions as Energizers

Figure 11-3

This activity provides practice in fine motor coordination, eye-hand coordination, auditory decoding, association, translation, organization, generalization, and integration.

Present the challenge to the children in your class of making a picture about something that really can't be seen. "There is a poem that starts like this," you begin.

> *Who has seen the wind?*
> *Neither I nor you . . .*

"We really can't see the wind, can we? Yet there are ways that we are able to tell when it is blowing. How?" you ask your students.

Use student ideas as energizers by taking them outside for a discussion about the wind. You might prefer to just look out the window or have the children recall their experiences with the wind. "We know that the wind is blowing from the sound it makes as it hums in the treetops or howls around corners," you continue. "What else tells us it is windy?" Students will say the trees toss their branches, papers flutter down the street, clothes flap wildly on the clothesline, and our own clothes blow against our legs.

Reach every individual by explaining that each child should choose one way in which he can see the wind. "Draw this on your paper and color it in brightly with crayons. When the drawings are finished, we will use paints for windy skies. Remember to show how the wind is affecting the person or object in your picture," you caution the class. "And things in the background should be blown about also. For example, if someone's skirt and hair is being blown behind them, flowers or shrubs in the drawing would be bending the same way. Only a tornado blows things in all directions at once!"

Appreciate each person as students start their windy pictures. Suggest that drawings be large enough to really show the work of the wind. Continue to use student ideas as energizers by sharing with the class examples of how some children have drawn figures bent and buffeted by the breeze. When the crayon work is complete, demonstrate how a watercolor wash is brushed across the sky. Some areas can be blotted up with a tissue or towel to suggest clouds sailing overhead. You may pass trays of watercolor to each child or have them take turns using diluted blue tempera at a painting station.

Looking at the wind is a success if the wax resist activity reflects your students' understanding of the rest of the poem about the wind.

> *Who has seen the wind?*
> *Neither I nor you:*
> *But when the leaves hang trembling,*
> *The wind is passing through.*
>
> *Who has seen the wind?*
> *Neither you nor I:*
> *But when the trees bow down their heads,*
> *The wind is passing by.*
>
> *Christina Rossetti*

Perhaps your students would like to write poems, too, about how they see the wind.

TEXTURE RUBBINGS

Materials needed: 12 × 18" colored construction paper, 8 × 12" manila paper, crayons, scissors, paste, and a scrap box containing such odds and ends as toothpicks, buttons, pieces of screen, cloth, or sandpaper. (See Figure 11-4.)

This activity provides practice in fine motor coordination, eye-hand coordination, auditory decoding, sequencing, associa-

Mini-Excursions as Energizers

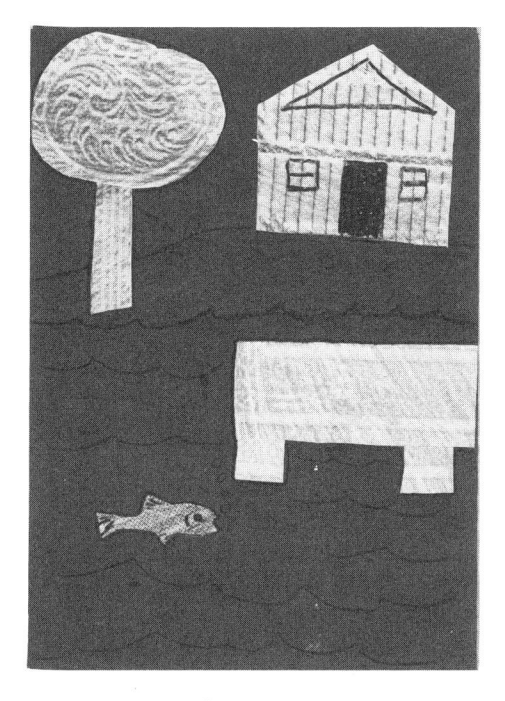

Figure 11-4

tion, translation, organization, generalization, and integration.

Present the challenge to each child in your creative class of collecting impressions of textures to combine in a cut paper picture. Prepare a few examples, yourself, before you begin the lesson. Hold small sheets of manila paper over such familiar things as an air vent, tile on the floor or around the sink, a cinder block, or even a ruler or scissors. Make impressions of the shape or texture of each object by rubbing the paper with the side of a crayon which has had the paper removed. Explain that shapes and textures may be printed by rubbing and show them your examples.

Use student ideas as energizers by having the children guess the sources of the texture rubbings that you made. Ask what some of the textures suggest. The square pattern of the grate may look like part of a brick building or it could be a checkered apron. The cinder block rubbing might suggest the fur of some animal or a wooly blanket or even desert sand! The ruler could be turned into a tall object like a very straight tree or a telephone pole. And the scissors do look like the beak of a round eyed bird!

Reach every individual by letting each child collect his own assortment of texture rubbings. This may be done right in the classroom using items from the scrapbox or you may take the children outside in order to get a greater variety of impressions. Give students several sheets of manila paper and crayons of different colors with paper wrappers removed. Dark ones are best. And remind the children to be thinking of what each texture they rub suggests.

Appreciate each person by explaining how to use the examples of different textures in a cut paper picture. Choose one texture, decide what it looks like, and cut it to the proper shape. Place it on the 12 × 18″ colored construction paper background, but don't paste it down until all the parts of the picture are arranged. Use the rest of the texture rubbings for the other parts of the picture. Cut them out, too, adding details with crayon. Encourage the students to share suggestions. Remember that a rubbing can suggest something quite different from its source. When the pictures have been thoughtfully composed, pass out the paste.

Texture rubbings are a success if using textures in an imaginative way results in interesting pictures. Gathering textures is a good energizer. Have each child give his work a one sentence title that contains a word describing a texture, such as soft, rough, or bumpy.

PACKAGE DESIGN

Materials needed: 8 × 12″ colored construction paper, 6 × 8″ pieces of white drawing paper, crayons, scissors, and paste or glue.

This activity provides practice in fine motor coordination, eye-hand coordination, auditory decoding, translation, organization, generalization, and integration.

Present the challenge to children in your class of becoming commercial artists and trying to sell a new brand of breakfast cereal. Point out that there are two types of art. **Fine art** can be paintings, drawings, prints, or sculpture which are done just because the artist wants to be creative. These works can be sold, but only because the buyer would enjoy having them to look at. **Commercial art** has a purpose and includes designing clothes and furniture, cartooning, creating advertisements, and designing packages. Explain how important it is

Mini-Excursions as Energizers

that food packages be attractive because there are so many products on the grocer's shelves that cans must be bright and eye catching to attract the shopper's attention. Take a trip to the grocery store with this in mind.

Use student ideas as energizers after your excursion by discussing the childrens' observations, especially concerning cereal. If it is not practical for you to actually visit a supermarket, you may rely on your students' experiences. You will find that even young children are experts on breakfast foods and familiar with the cereal section of stores! "Which packages did you like the most at the market?" you ask. "Yes, those that were colorful with bright and easy to read letters. What did you notice about the names of cereals?" you continue. "Right! Most of them were funny ones that would appeal to children. Do you think that names are important to cereals? Can you think of some new ones?"

Reach every individual as the children become interested in naming breakfast foods. Continue to use their ideas as energizers by listening to the many names and slogans that they think of. "Smile! The cereal that makes you happy all day. Rockets! A bowlful sends you out of this world. Firecrackers! The flavor that explodes in your mouth." Your students are sure to have plenty of suggestions on this subject!

Appreciate each person by giving everyone the chance to put his idea on paper. Explain that the 8 × 12" colored construction paper will represent the cereal box. Students are to draw an eye catching illustration on the 6 × 8" white drawing paper and color it brightly with crayons. This should be mounted on the "box," or construction paper. The letters of the cereal's name will then be cut from colored construction paper. A good way to do this is to take a two inch strip just the right length to go across the paper and cut it into as many rectangles as there are letters in the title. Any letter can easily be cut from a rectangle. In this way, all letters will be uniform in size and fit the paper perfectly. Demonstrate this process for your class. (See Figure 11-5.) Finally, students should add the slogan selected to the package design with crayon.

Designing packages is a success if your directions enable each child to design an original and attractive package and the class learns about fine and commercial art. Display the designs. If they were really boxes at the market, kids would clamor for them!

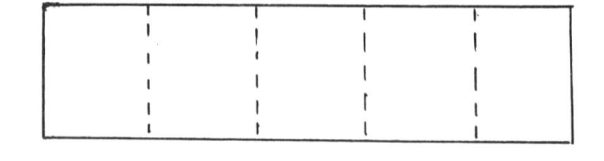

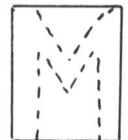

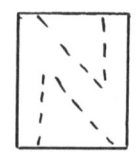

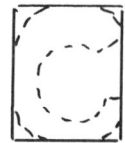

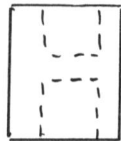

Figure 11-5

GETTING TO KNOW A TREE

Materials needed: 12 × 18" manila paper, black crayons, water color paints, brushes, newspapers, and paper towels. (See Figure 11-6.)

This activity provides practice in fine motor coordination, eye-hand coordination, association, translation, organization, generalization, and integration.

Present the challenge to each child in your class of becoming completely familiar with a certain tree through the seasons of the year. This mini-excursion should be repeated several times during the year. Begin in the fall by taking your class outside to the playground or a park. Have each choose a tree which will be "his" to study and draw for the rest of the year. Each student should have manila drawing paper, a black crayon, and a workbook or sheet of cardboard to support his paper as he draws.

Use student ideas as energizers before the children go to work by generalizing observations. They will notice that tree trunks are thicker at the bottom and become more slender as the tree stretches up towards the sun. And the limbs, too, are wider where they begin and thinner at their ends. Each tree has many branches growing from it, tapering to fine twigs. Every type of tree has leaves of a special shape and bark rough in texture. The roots of the tree can be seen as they begin to push into the earth for nourishment.

Figure 11-6

Reach every individual by moving among the children as they put their observations on paper. If a child is having trouble, perhaps he should choose a tree of simpler shape with fewer branches. Or maybe you can help him by pointing out the shape of the trunk, the positions of the limbs, and the contour of the leaves. Emphasize that he need not draw every twig and leaf. When most of the children have finished their drawings, return to your classroom to finish the project.

Appreciate each person with your compliments on a drawing job well done. Let students complete any unfinished work and be sure that all have used their black crayon heavily enough, for the next step is adding fall colors to the tree with watercolor paints. You may pass paints to each individual or have them take turns working with the paints at a painting station during their spare time. Only a small amount of water and a little paint are needed to suggest bright fall foliage. Too much might spoil the effect of the crayon drawings.

Getting to know a tree is a success if the children have fun discussing trees in general and are able to draw one tree in particular. They are already looking forward to studying the tree during the next season. A stark winter tree might be sketched in charcoal. In spring, pens could be used for drawing the fine details of budding leaves, or your class might prefer to portray soft spring colors with pastels!

STUDYING SHADOWS

Materials needed: 12 × 18″ white drawing paper, 8 × 12″ manila paper, 8 × 12″ black construction paper, crayons, scissors, and paste. (See Figure 11-7.)

Figure 11-7

This activity provides practice in eye-hand coordination, fine motor coordination, auditory decoding, verbal endings, association, translation, organization, generalization, and integration.

Present the challenge to the children in your class of making a mini-excursion to the playground on a sunny morning in order to discover more about shadows. The best time for this activity is early on a bright day when shadows are dark and long.

Have them stand with their backs to the sun so that they may observe their shadows. Ask them to notice the height of the sun in the sky.

Use student ideas as energizers by asking how the location of the sun affects shadows. Be sure that they are aware that when the sun is low in the sky, shadows are longer. They will be just as long at sundown as at sunrise. At noon when the sun is high, they almost disappear! Shadows are fun! Each of us has one that copies all our antics!

Reach every individual with the pleasure of a poem when you return to the classroom:

"I have a little shadow that goes in and out with me,
And what can be the use of him is more than I can see.
He is very, very like me from the heels up to the head;
And I see him jump before me when I jump into my bed.

The funniest thing about him is the way he likes to grow—
Not at all like proper children, which is always very slow;
For sometimes he shoots up taller like an India-rubber ball,
And sometimes he gets so little that there's none of him at all.

He hasn't got a notion of how children ought to play,
And can only make a fool of me in every sort of way.
He stays so close beside me, he's a coward you can see;
I'd think shame to stick to nursie as that shadow sticks to me.

One morning very early, before the sun was up,
I rose and found the shining dew on every buttercup;
But my lazy little shadow, like an errant sleepyhead,
Had stayed at home behind me and was fast asleep in bed.

Robert Louis Stevenson

"Now we can understand what this poem means. It would be fun to make some pictures about shadows, too," you suggest.

Appreciate each person by having everyone draw a picture of himself on 8 × 12" manila paper. In these self-portraits each child should be doing something that he enjoys like throwing a ball, dancing, running, or just jumping around. Remind students that knees and elbows must bend when they move! Finish the pictures by coloring them with crayons and placing them on top of the black construction paper. Holding both pieces of paper together, cut the figures out. Paste the self-portraits near the top of the white drawing paper. Shadows, of course, should be pasted upside down, feet touching those of the crayon figure and heading in the same direction.

Making pictures of shadows is a success if seeing their shadows in the early morning sun is a happy way for your students to start the day and each one makes a self-portrait of a favorite activity. As a follow-up, each student might enjoy writing a poem about something special that his shadow did.

OUR NEIGHBORHOOD MURAL

Materials needed: 8 × 12" colored construction paper, a project roll or shelf paper, scissors, and glue.

This activity provides practice in fine motor coordination, eye-hand coordination, translation, organization, generalization, and integration.

Present the challenge to your class of exploring the neighborhood near your school, then making a mural of their discoveries. Take your students on a walk up and down the street or road on either side of the school. Caution the children to really notice the buildings that they pass since they will be making pictures of them when they return. Encourage them to point out interesting or unusual observations to their classmates as they walk along.

Use student ideas as energizers by having the children recall what they saw and make a list of the sights on the chalkboard. Listing buildings in the proper order will help in organizing the mural when the time comes. What were some of the details students noticed about these buildings? And should things like trees or phone booths be included in the mural? The list becomes an experience chart for reading in a very young class.

Reach every individual by letting each one choose a building to make a picture about. On a city block, there should be buildings enough for every child. If your setting is a rural one, however, you may find that you need to vary the assignments by having several children work on one set of buildings. For example, one child could make the house, another the barn, and others the rest of a farm's outbuildings. Farm machinery and other vehicles could be included in a list that contains only a few buildings.

Mini-Excursions as Energizers

Appreciate each person once the subjects have been selected by explaining how every child can make his part of the mural. Unroll the project paper along a wall of the classroom. If space is a problem, the paper could go under your chalkboard or on the wall in the hall outside your room. Every building will be made from 8 × 12″ construction paper of the appropriate color. Point out that the rectangular paper is almost the right shape for many buildings. It can be cut in two across the length for a long, low building or turned vertically for a tall one. Windows, doors, and the right roof should be added from colored paper scraps. Encourage each child to remember the basic shape of the building he is making. And don't forget details like signs, awnings, or window boxes! When each child has cut his construction paper to the correct shape and added scrap paper details, help him glue his building in its proper place on the mural paper.

Our neighborhood mural is a success if each child completes one part of the picture and places it properly with the help of the list on your chalkboard. What is needed to complete the picture? Sure! Trees, traffic, and people. These can be added later when children have spare time. Everyone is proud of the mural and pleased as he shares in the work and fun.

Chapter 12

Describing Experiences Visually

A VERY BAD BLIZZARD

Materials needed: 12 × 18" blue construction paper, white tempera paint, brushes, newspapers to covers desks, and crayons. (See Figure 12-1.)

This activity provides practice in fine motor coordination, eye-hand coordination, association, translation, organization, generalization, and integration.

Present the challenge to each child in your class of reexperiencing the worst blizzard that he can remember, then making a picture about it.

Use student ideas as energizers by having the children take turns telling about "pictures" in their memories of very bad blizzards. Snow blowing and drifting high as the eves on a house and covering windows, father shoveling a path through the

Figure 12-1

deep snow to the road, plows pushing the snow into mountains on either side of the street, and crews in power trucks working to restore electricity are usually among the responses. Other children have recollections of wading through waist deep snow or gliding down hills on flying saucers or toboggans as they took advantage of a day off from school.

Reach every individual by having each one draw the experience that he has in mind on blue construction paper with crayons. Color it brightly. Remember to include all the important details except the snow. That will be added last of all with white paint and brushes. Work large enough so that everything can be clearly seen. One idea or experience is probably all that should be put in each picture.

Appreciate each person by showing your interest in every idea. That is an unbeatable energizer! Point out that pictures should be drawn near the center of the paper. If drawing is done too close to the bottom, there will be no room to paint on the deep snow. Remind them again that all crayon work should be bright and heavy. Otherwise, the picture might be hidden when the tempera snow is added. Snow surely covers many things, but it should not hide the child's idea! When the crayon work is complete, have the students take turns using brushes and paint at a painting station in your room, or give them each materials to finish the project at their desks. With a few whisks of a brush, snow whirls around people and buildings, and flecks of white paint become flakes of snow falling from the sky!

Describing a bad blizzard is a success if each child turns a memory into a picture. All the wonder of winter is in your room as you display the pictures. If you live in an area where tropical storms rather than blizzards are a seasonal occurrence, you may use the same approach to painting. Vary the process by having students work on white paper and use a blue watercolor wash for waves and rain.

A BIG YELLOW BUS RIDE

Materials needed: 12 × 18″ yellow construction paper, scissors, glue, and crayons. (See Figure 12-2A.)

Figure 12-2A

This activity provides practice in fine motor coordination, eye-hand coordination, auditory decoding, translation, organization, generalization, and integration.

Present the challenge to your class of making some extraordinary pictures about a very ordinary experience. Most students ride

200   Imagination and Environment as Energizers

buses to get to school each day. Everyone rides school buses during activities such as field trips. Boys and girls are really experts on this subject!

Use student ideas as energizers by encouraging some of the children to share their impressions of a bus ride with the others. They will observe that the bus is quite crowded by the time it reaches school (each seat is filled) and it is rather noisy. They enjoy talking to friends and sometimes the bus driver plays the radio. Sometimes they all sing songs. One may point out that country roads can be very bumpy!

Reach every individual by explaining that the school bus pictures will be made on 12 × 18″ yellow construction paper. A school bus is very long. We can show this by cutting off a strip two or three inches wide from the length of the paper. What remains will be the body of the bus. The front end, tires, and fenders can be cut from the scraps and glued in place. Round off a few corners and your long school bus shape is finished! (See Figure 12-2B.) "Now, pretend that we can see right inside the

Figure 12-2B

Describing Experiences Visually

bus. Draw the driver and the steering wheel, the seats, and all the passengers on the bus—right on the bus! That's what we call an 'X-ray' picture," you point out.

Appreciate each person as the big, yellow buses are cut out and glued together. Impressions of energy and activity emerge as children make their crayon pictures. The happy faces in some reflect a good time. Others show a somewhat harried bus driver. And a few children include conversations in comic strip style "clouds" over heads. One individual even draws an X-ray view of the engine!

Making pictures of a big, yellow bus ride is a success if every student has something to say on the subject and knows just how to say it. You will want to display these pictures where people can enjoy them. They are sure to cause comments—and smiles!

BRIGHT LIGHTS AT NIGHT

Materials needed: 12 × 18" black construction paper, crayons, and yellow chalk. (See Figure 12-3.)

This activity provides practice in fine motor coordination, eye-

Figure 12-3

hand coordination, association, translation, organization, generalization, and integration.

Present the challenge to every student in your class of recapturing on paper something special that he saw at night. "Everything looks quite different at night," you begin. "Even things that are familiar take on an air of mystery because of the darkness that surrounds us. Especially interesting are objects that appear in the glow of a light. One simple example might be the front door of your house or apartment. You have seen it countless times, but at night when your porch light is on, it looks particularly warm and inviting. Can you think of some other examples?"

Use student ideas as energizers as children respond with such ideas as a ship coming into harbor, a lighthouse, or a long pier with boats tied up for the night. A child from the city might mention the storefront of the delicatessen across the street or his friends playing under a street lamp. A country child could recall the headlights on the hay truck as it returns from the fields on a hot summer night or the headlights on a lone car driving along a dark road. Exciting experiences make good motivators, too, like the lights on the ferris wheel at the fair or the glow from a campfire at a beach party.

Reach every individual after suggestions have been shared by explaining that 12 × 18" black construction paper will be the background. Draw the special thing and its light big and bright on the paper with crayons. Use yellow chalk to show how the glow from the light spreads out into the night.

Appreciate every person by helping individuals who need a review of suggestions or questions about some of the special things which are seen at night. Point out that in some cases, people or objects near the light can be seen in the background, but we are mostly concerned with just one idea in each picture. The drawings take on a glow as warmth is added to each picture with yellow chalk.

Picturing bright lights at night is a success if focusing on just one idea helps the students to develop it in detail. Now why not give your class a chance to stretch vocabularies by having each student write a descriptive sentence to title his drawing?

Describing Experiences Visually 203

MY ROOM

Materials needed: 12 × 18" white drawing paper, colored construction paper, cloth scraps, scissors, crayons, and paste. (See Figure 12-4.)

This activity provides practice in fine motor coordination, eye-hand coordination, sequencing, translation, organization, generalization, and integration.

Figure 12-4

Present the challenge to each child in your class of reproducing a part of his room on paper. Point out that although his home may not be the most elegant or fancy one in the world, it is still a very special place. Most of us feel that way particularly about our own room. It is where we have our toys and hobbies, where we bring our friends, or where we can be alone if we feel like it.

Use student ideas as energizers as you discuss with the class some of the things that might be included in the pictures. "Let's each try to remember how just one side of our room looks.

Can someone describe his room for us?" A child answers that there is a bed, a bureau, and a chair along one wall of his room. "Is there a window in the wall?" you ask. "And what is on your bureau? What kind of a chair is it? Do you have a rug or toys on your floor? Is there a bedspread with stripes or some other pattern on it?"

Reach every individual by showing the class the materials from which the pictures will be made and explaining that 12 × 18" white paper will represent one side of the room. Draw a line with a ruler across the paper, almost halfway up. This will be the line where the wall meets the floor of the room. Objects against the wall should be placed on that line. Things on the floor or in the foreground must be placed beneath the line, closer to the bottom edge of the paper. Furniture, toys, lamps, or other objects can be drawn on colored construction paper, then cut out and pasted in place. A window in the wall, or a pattern on the wallpaper, may be drawn and colored with crayon. Cloth scraps may be used for curtains, rugs, or even clothes on hooks or chairs.

Appreciate each person by giving everyone a chance to select a few pieces of colored construction paper and cloth scraps to get started. Be sure that everyone begins by dividing the paper with a horizontal line. Some child may require help with proportions; older students are anxious for more realism. Suggest that the largest object be drawn and cut out first. The next largest thing should be done next and so on. This will aid in establishing the proper relationship among furnishings. You will discover that younger groups are not likely to be worried about such matters. A small child typically makes the thing which is most important to him the biggest and is happy with it. Thus proportion needn't be emphasized. Let the student response be your guide as you help individuals.

Pictures of my room are a success if each child is able to respond in a personal way to the problem you presented. These pictures would fit well in a folder of student work to be sent home or might be fun for parents to find on their child's desk at an open house.

A TERRIFIC TASTE

Materials needed: 12 × 18" colored construction paper, 8 × 12" flesh colored construction paper, colored paper scraps, scissors, and paste. (See Figure 12-5.)

Describing Experiences Visually

Figure 12-5

This activity provides practice in fine motor coordination, eye-hand coordination, association, translation, organization, generalization, and integration.

Present the challenge to the gourmets in your class of showing in a picture how they felt when they tasted something terrific. Ask them to remember a time when they ate something that really made an impression on them. It might have been delicious, or it could have been so strange and unpleasant that it was hard to swallow.

Use student ideas as energizers by having children tell about memorable tastes and their reactions to them. Pizza, ice cream cones, and watermelon are foods that most people like a lot. Ask how their faces looked when they bit into a cool, juicy slice of watermelon. Let a child demonstrate. "What about sour tastes?" you continue. "How does your expression change when you suck a wedge of lemon?" You are sure to find that another child is eager to pantomime the experience. Did you realize how much food can affect our faces?

Reach every individual by explaining how each one can use colored construction paper to describe a delicious dish—or a bitter bite. "The 12 × 18" colored paper will be the background. We will also each have two sheets of 8 × 12" paper nearly the color of our skin. From one piece we will cut the shape of our head. As you know, this should be oval or egg shaped. Try to make it almost as large as the paper so that it will show up well," you suggest. "Trace your hand on the other piece in a position that appears to be holding food. Paste the head on the paper and the hand coming out from the edge towards the mouth. That will be the basic beginning for each picture, but the details will be very different!"

Appreciate each person by helping every individual to show his experience by using colored paper scraps to make the eyes, nose, mouth, hair, and even the food that is being eaten. Remind them that you discussed and demonstrated making mouths at sour tastes. Eyes reflect feelings, too. Urge them to show this in their pictures.

Picturing a memorable taste is a success if each child uses cut paper to tell about a bite that was either tempting or terrible. Have each child give his work a one sentence title which uses a word to describe a taste sensation, such as "My ice cream cone was cold and creamy." It might be fun to display these in your cafeteria!

A HAPPY CROWD

Materials needed: 12 × 18" manila paper, colored construction paper, scissors, crayons and paste. (See Figure 12-6.)

This activity provides practice in fine motor coordination, eye-hand coordination, auditory decoding, sequencing, association, translation, organization, generalization, and integration.

Present the challenge to each student of re-creating on paper the impressions that he once had when he was in a happy crowd. "It's always a good time when we get together with our family and friends for special occasions, isn't it?" you point out. "It seems that we enjoy ourselves more because we can share our fun with those around us!"

Use student ideas as energizers as some of the children recall and describe a pleasant memory such as going to a parade with colorful floats and many marching groups, or a football game with cheerleaders and the program at half-time, or even re-

Describing Experiences Visually 207

cess on the playground when we all seem to think of so many things to do!

Reach every individual by explaining an easy but effective way of making a lively picture just full of people. "It would take a long time for us to draw each person in a large group such as a parade, wouldn't it?" you begin. "Instead, we will try to suggest the activity and give an impression of all that is happening. We will each have two sheets of 12 × 18″ manila paper and some colored construction paper. One sheet of the manila paper will be our background. Choose a time when you were in a happy crowd. Next, pick out three or four things that people were doing. For example, from a parade you could select a majorette, a flag bearer, a drummer, and a trumpet player. On the second sheet of manila paper, draw pictures of each of the three or four people 'doing his thing.' You needn't arrange them as if they are playing together, because after you color them you will cut them out," you explain.

Appreciate each person by encouraging every child as he begins to draw. If one has drawing problems suggest that he begin by sketching a stick man, then adding clothing and details. This approach is described in Chapter 1, Catching the Action. When most students are finished with their drawings, explain

Figure 12-6

that two or three pieces of colored construction paper should be put under each figure as it is cut out. This will result in identical shapes or silhouettes for each activity. Arrange these on the background. Overlap the figures to fit them all on the paper. This will also help give the effect of many people and a lot going on! Start near the top with the silhouettes, then work down, pasting the original figure drawings in the foreground. Add any details needed in the background with crayon to complete the pictures.

Making pictures of happy crowds is a success if most students follow directions and fill the pages with fun. A pleasant personal experience is always a good energizer! When you display the pictures, everyone can see that they reflect two characteristics of elementary classrooms—energy and activity!

GOING FAST

Materials needed: 12 × 18" colored construction paper, crayons, yarn and cloth scraps, scissors, and glue. (See Figure 12-7.)

This activity provides practice in fine motor coordination, eye-hand coordination, association, translation, organization, generalization, and integration.

Present the challenge to the fast-moving youngsters in your class of showing speed in some special pictures. "It can be a lot of fun to go fast. We know that speeding on bikes and in cars is very dangerous and that traffic rules must be obeyed," you warn. "Yet there are many times that we can safely enjoy the thrill of motion."

Use student ideas as energizers in a lively class discussion about good times the children had going fast. Usually you will find that they are anxious to describe the excitement of rides at fairs that whirl and spin rapidly, or riding bikes or minibikes, or zooming over the snow in snowmobiles in winter. And the joy of running fast is something that we all can easily experience!

Reach every individual by helping each visualize the effect of motion. Ask how someone looks when he is going fast. Students will observe that hair is blown back and clothing billows behind. Feelings are reflected in faces. Often we can see that the person is really hanging on tight.

Appreciate every person as each one draws a picture of a special speedy experience on 12 × 18" colored construction paper.

Figure 12-7

Remind one student to make his picture large enough to include all the details just mentioned. Urge another to color his drawing brightly with crayons. Yarn can be glued in place for hair streaming out behind. Colorful cloth scraps can be clothing blowing and flapping.

Making pictures about going fast is a success if every child has an experience from which to draw and captures it vividly on paper. While children are still involved with the subject, why not take advantage of their enthusiasm and use it as an energizer in your language program? Short stories or paragraphs could be written about the fun of going fast.

A SUDDEN SHOWER

Materials needed: 12 × 18″ manila or white drawing paper cut into 8 × 16″ paper on the paper cutter, crayons, light blue tempera paint, and brushes. (See Figure 12-8.)

This activity provides practice in fine motor coordination, eye-hand coordination, auditory decoding, association, translation, organization, generalization, and integration.

Present the challenge to your children of catching someone or something in a shower of tempera paint. "Sudden showers can be a pleasant surprise," you begin. "If the day is sweltering hot, rain brings cooling relief. But sometimes an unexpected cloudburst can be a problem," you continue. "If you are away from home without a raincoat or umbrella, you might get soaking wet!"

Use student ideas as energizers that help each child select a subject to catch in his shower picture. "What else might be affected by a surprise shower besides ourselves?" you ask. "And would the effect be bad or good?" Answers may include flowers that lift leaves and blossoms towards the refreshing drops or people on motorcycles caught in a cloudburst or picnickers that scramble for shelter. Creatures in the woods could use trees as an umbrella!

Reach every individual and hold his interest by suggesting that his ideas can be the beginning of an unusual picture if he draws a cloud at the top of the long piece of paper. It can be a crowd of angry storm clouds that holds a real downpour or just a little rain cloud that brings a few sprinkles. Next, near the bottom of the paper, draw whatever is caught in the sudden shower. Be sure to make the picture large enough to show up well and color it brightly.

Figure 12-8

Describing Experiences Visually

Appreciate each person as the children put their ideas down on paper. Some children choose to give their clouds personalities, drawing them with angry or mischievous faces. As a few students complete their pictures, explain and demonstrate how the tempera "shower" should be created. Paint may be brushed on the paper—over the cloud at the top and in puddles at the bottom. Then the brush is dipped lightly in the paint and gently tapped across a finger, sending drops of paint onto the paper beneath. That becomes a sudden shower!

Pictures of a sudden shower are a success if students are able to organize their drawings to express their ideas clearly. Drawing about the mischief made by rain is a good energizer. Nobody appreciates a prank more than children! These showery pictures would look attractive mounted on 12 × 18" colored construction paper. And they would make a good display for your room especially in April—a month noted for showers!

Keeping Up the Good Work with Imagination and Environment

There are lots of ways that the preceeding activities can be varied to meet the needs of your particular class or individuals in that class as you keep up the good work. For example, puppets can be made in minutes! Dancing finger puppets can easily emerge from small sheets of oak tag or cardboard. The character is drawn, colored brightly, cut out, and two holes for fingers cut from the bottom. Or use a little box or a scrap of paper rolled into a cylinder for puppet heads. Features are drawn on or cut from paper and pasted in place. These quick and easy puppets can be completed with a piece of cloth glued inside of the head. The cloth suggests a body and conceals the hand of the puppeteer. A puppet is as close as your scrap box!

Mask making methods are many, too! For a real touch of drama, start with 18 × 24" colored construction paper and cut away only enough to achieve the desired shape for a face. Add bigger than life features from bright cut paper. Or try putting down the contours and colors of a face with pieces of colored tissue paper pasted in place and brushing them with diluted white glue. When this is dry, draw on details with felt-tip markers. These are both unusual masks for display. An easy mask for wearing is made from a strip of oak tag approximately 6 × 18". Cut a triangle at the lower edge for a nose, holes on either side for eyes, and add ears or horns or whiskers and other distinguishing features. Wrap this around the top of the child's head "Lone Ranger" style.

Wondrous worlds beyond those mentioned in Chapter 9 exist in your students' imaginations. Continue to explore them with your class. Have each person imagine that he is a leaf tossed high in the sky or a bird flying south for the winter. What does he see? Music can be a great energizer, too. What pictures do portions of "The New World Symphony" or "Dance Macabre" bring to mind? Or go undersea to the Beatles' "Octopuses Garden." Let the students finger paint to music, too, eliciting rhythmic patterns in paint. If you have no finger paint paper, butcher or freezer paper will do. No paint? Spread liquid starch over the paper and add a teaspoon of tempera. Have the children draw with pencils or markers, using their rulers and only straight lines. The world looks different with no curves allowed! Crayon etching takes time but is an enjoyable way to exercise the imagination. Paper is covered entirely with bright splotches of heavy crayon color. A thick coating of black crayon is added. Etch a bright picture into the black crayon by scraping it away with the point of a pair of scissors or a nail file.

Keep up the good work of expanding awareness by challenging students to describe feeling with paints or chalks. Help them to compare the qualities and intensities of colors and emotions before they make the moody pictures. Or it could be interesting to use photos of flowers (in a seed catalog, perhaps) as the basis for patterns. Have each child choose a flower, simplify its shape and copy its color, repeating it over and over on bright paper. And speaking of flowers, why not have students do detail drawings from life of flowers, roots and all, and label the parts when studying plants in science? Such a direct experience might be more meaningful than copying a chart from a book.

Don't forget, either, the many opportunities for mini-excursions right in your school. The flaming furnace in the boiler room or the huge potato masher in the kitchen are things which children find fascinating. The gym provides a perfect chance to appreciate people in action. Try letting your class practice gesture drawing (Chapter 1) there, using black crayons or markers. Or turn it into a tactile experience by having them describe the movements by gluing yarn to oak tag or by bending pipe cleaners.

Allow time after special learning experiences for students to describe their impressions visually by drawing. This will help each individual to assimilate and retain his new knowledge.

As you continue your expeditions into the world of fantasy and your explorations of the environment, individual responses will be wonderful energizers for your students. The learning experiences along the road to artistic maturity can be exciting and happy adventures!

Index

A

African masks, 142, 143
American Indian masks, 142, 143
Animals:
    cardboard carton, 72-74
    huge cut paper, 149-151
    scrapwood, 61-63
    torn paper, 79-81
Announcements, 114
Aquarium wax resist pictures, 173-174
Armature, 69-70
Art, commercial and fine, 188
Awareness activities:
    aquarium wax resist pictures, 173-174
    center designs in nature, 170-171
    cut paper fish, 165-167
    detail drawing of room, 176-177
    happy faces, 171-173
    painting a pet, 174-176
    patterns in nature, 168-169
    scrapwood surprises, 177-179
    self-portraits, 167-168

B

Background, 85
Bag:
    masks, 137-138
    puppet pals, 119-121
Balloons, papier-mâché over, 144-146
Birds, light bulb, 68-70
Blizzard, picture, 197-199
Blowing tempera paint, 31, 33
Bookcovers, 50

Bottles:
    drawings, 26
    people, 65-68
Bowl of fruit, drawing, 26
Brushes, 38-40, 114
Bus ride, picture, 199-201

C

Candlesticks, drawing, 26
Cardboard and foil reliefs, 70-72
Cardboard carton creatures, 72-74
Cards, Christmas, 52-54
Cartons, creatures, 72-74
Center designs in nature, 170-171
Chalks, 114
Character heads, 63-65
Charcoal, drawing round or cylindrical objects, 17
Christmas cards, 52-54
Circus masks, 144-146
Clay, puppets, 128-129
Cloth, puppets, 124-126, 128-129
Cloth and crayon creatures, 158-159
Collage, 93-95
Collage visages, 146-148
Color:
    creating depth, 85-87
    learning about, 114
    mixing, 37-38
Commercial art, 188
Compositions, newspaper, 93-95
Concepts, formation, 5, 117
Continuous line drawings, 28-29
Contour drawings, 15-17

217

Index

Coordination, 5
Copies of art work, 114
Costumes, drawings, 20
Crayon and cloth creatures, 158-159
Crayon and finger paint, 161-163
Crayons:
    continuous line drawings, 28
    figure drawing, 20
    plant drawings, 15
    prints, 114
    still life drawings, 26
    texture drawings, 28
Creative energy, 5
Creatures:
    cardboard carton, 72-74
    cloth and crayon, 158-159
    folded paper, 130-131
"Cross section," 170-171
Crowd, picture, 206-208
Cut paper animals, 149-151
Cut paper fish, 165-167
Cylinder masks, 139-141
Cylindrical objects, drawing, 17

D

Demonstration, 113
Depth:
    background, 85
    brightest color, 85
    closest object, 85
    foreground, 85
    horizon, 85
    illusion of space, 87
    lightest color, 86
    size and color, 85-87
    smallest object, 86
Designs:
    package, 188-190
    repeated shapes, 89-90
Detail:
    drawings of room, 176-177
    emphasizing, 40-42
Detail line drawings, 19-20
Dimension, 63
Direct experience, 118
Directions, modify, 113
"Dissect," 170, 171
Distance, 85
Distant planet, 154-156
Donald Duck, 64
Drama, 117

Drawings:
    black tempera paint, 22
    bottles, 26
    bowl of fruit, 26
    candlesticks, 26
    charcoal, 17
    continuous line, 28-29
    contour, 15-17
    costumes, 20
    cylindrical objects, 17
    detail line, 19-20
    figure, 20-22
    fish, 28
    gesture, 22-24
    highlight, 17
    markers, 24, 28
    musical instruments, 19
    oil pastels or crayons, 15, 20, 24, 26, 28
    pens, 19, 24
    plants, 15, 26
    room details, 176-177
    round objects, 17-18
    still life, 26-27
    texture, 24-26

E

Egg, 152-154
Egg cartons, 113-114
Environment:
    awareness, 5
    energizer, 117-118
Eskimo masks, 142, 143
Evaluation, 6
Excursions:
    looking at the wind, 184-186
    neighborhood mural, 194-195
    package design, 188-190
    sounds while sitting, 183-184
    studying shadows, 192-194
    texture rubbings, 186-188
    tree, 190-192
    wonderful weeds, 181-183

F

Faces:
    happy, 171-173
    with feeling, 146-148
Figure drawings, 20-22
Figures, foil, 74-76
Fine art, 188

Index

Finger paint, 161-163
Fingerprints, 54
Finger puppets, sawdust, 132-133
Fish:
    cut paper, 165-167
    drawing, 28
Fixative, 114
Foil and cardboard reliefs, 70-72
Foil figures, 74-76
Folded paper creatures, 130-131
Footprints, 54
Foreground, 85
Foxes, 73
Free-form shape, 152
Fruit, drawing, 26

G

Gadgets, 114
Geometric shapes, 74, 114
Gesture drawing, 22-24
Giraffes, 73
Going fast, 208-209

H

Hand puppets:
    papier-mâché and cloth, 124-126
    stocking, 121-123
Happy faces, 171-173
Heads, character, 63-65
Highlights, drawings, 17
Hippos, 73
Holiday greetings, 114
Horizon, 85
Huge cut paper animals, 149-151

I

Imagination, 117
Indian shields, 81-83
Individualized awareness activities, 165-179 (*see also* Awareness activities)
Individualized learning, 5
Ink, prints, 50-52
Instruments, musical, 19
Inventions, 159-161
Invitations, 114

L

Leaf prints, 45-47
Life, painting from, 110-111

Light and bright, 35
Light bulb birds, 68-70
Lights, night, 201-202
Line drawings:
    continuous, 28-29
    detail, 19-20
Lion, head, 61-62

M

Markers:
    continuous line drawings, 28
    texture drawings, 24
Masks:
    African, 142, 143
    American Indian, 142, 143
    circus, 144-146
    collage visages, 146-148
    cylinder, 139-141
    Eskimo, 142-143
    faces with feeling, 146-148
    paper bag, 137-139
    paper plate, 135-137
    papier-mâché, 141-144
    papier-mâché over balloons, 144-146
    primitive, 141-144
Media, 5
Mickey Mouse, 64
Mini-excursions, 181-195 (*see also* Excursions)
Montages:
    absurd, 156-158
    animated cartoons, 84
    good composition, 158
    individual's interests, 84
    magazine pictures, 83, 84, 156, 157
    motion, 83-85
    overlapping, 84-85, 157
    parts outlined, 157
    repeat shapes, 157
    write stories about, 158
Mosaics, paper, 114
Motivation, 6
Mural, neighborhood, 194-195
Musical instruments, drawing, 19

N

Nature:
    center designs, 170-171
    patterns, 168-169
Neighborhood mural, 194-195

Index

Newspaper compositions, 93-95
Night lights, picture, 201-202

O

Oak tag:
    Christmas card, 52-54
    print, 54
Oatmeal containers, 76-78
Oil pastels:
    brighter, 114
    continuous line drawings, 28
    figure drawing, 20
    not powdery, 115
    plant drawings, 15
    still life drawing, 26
    texture drawings, 24

P

Package design, 188-190
Painting:
    blowing tempera, 31-33
    color mixing, 37-38
    emphasizing detail, 40-42
    gadgets, 115
    large brushes, 38-40
    life, 110-111
    pet, 174-176
    portraits, 42
    stick, 33-35
    tempera and sponge, 35-37
Paper:
    animals, 149-151
    animated cartoons, 84
    collage, 93-95
    cutting, 114
    depth with size and color, 85-87
    designs with repeated shapes, 89-90
    fish, 165-167
    folded, creatures, 130-131
    Indian shields, 81-83
    mosaics, 114
    motion montages, 83-85
    newspaper compositions, 93-95
    oak tag, 52-54, 54-56
    sculpting, 115
    tissue, prints, 58-60
    torn, scenes, 79-81
    transparent tissue windows, 90-93
    wallpaper still lifes, 87-89
    wet, working on, 107-109

Paper bag:
    masks, 137-138
    puppet pals, 119-121
Paper cups, 114
Paper plate masks, 135-137
Papier-mâché:
    bottle people, 65-68
    character heads, 63-65
    circus masks, 144-146
    hand puppets, 124-126
    primitive masks, 141-144
Pastels, 114
Patterns, nature, 168-169
Pens:
    detail line drawings, 19
    texture drawings, 24
People, bottle, 65-68
Perception, 117
Personal expression, 117
Personality in portraits, 43
Personal response, 118
Pets:
    painting, 174-176
    torn paper, 79-81
Pictures:
    acquarium wax resist, 173-174
    big yellow bus ride, 199-201
    blizzard, 197-199
    bright lights at night, 201-202
    going fast, 208-209
    happy crowd, 206-208
    my room, 203-204
    still life, 26-27, 87-89
    sudden shower, 209-211
    terrific taste, 204-206
Planet, distant, 154-156
Plants:
    contour drawing, 15
    still life drawing, 26
Popsicle sticks:
    painting with, 33
    puppets, 128-129
Portraits:
    painting, 42-44
    self-, 167-168
    three-dimensional, 63
    watercolor, 105-107
Potato, prints, 47-50
Primary colors, 38
Primitive masks, 141-144
Prints:
    bookcovers, 50
    Christmas cards, 52-54
    coin, 51
    copies of art work, 114

Index

Prints *(cont.)*
    crayons, 114
    finger and foot, 54
    gadgets, 114
    leaf, 45-47
    oak tag, 54-56
    oak tag and string, 52-54
    part of picture, 50
    potato, 47-50
    relief, 56
    repeated printing, 50
    seasonal, 50-52
    stencil silhouette, 56-58
    styrofoam, 50-52
    tempera, 114
    tissue paper, 58
    wrapping paper, 50
Problems, anticipate, 113
Program covers, 114
Puppets:
    clay, cloth, Popsicle stick, 128-129
    cloth hand, 124-126
    folded paper creatures, 130-131
    paper bag, 119-121
    papier-mâché, 124-126
    sawdust finger, 132-133
    stocking hand, 121-123
    stuffed storybook, 126-128

R

Rain forest, watercolor, 107-109
Rain showers, 209-211
Relief:
    foil and cardboard, 70-72
    prints, 56
Repetition, shapes, 89-90
Response, personal, 118
Retention, 5
Room, picture of, 203-204
Room details, drawing, 176-177
Round objects:
    drawing, 26
    foil and cardboard reliefs, 70-72
Rubbings, texture, 186-188

S

Sawdust finger puppets, 132-133
Scenes, torn paper, 79-81
Scrapwood:
    animals, 61-63
    surprises, 177-179

Sculpture:
    animals in zoo, 73-74
    armature, 69
    cardboard carton creatures, 72-74
    dimension, 63
    foil and cardboard reliefs, 70-72
    foil figures, 74-76
    light bulb birds, 68-70
    lion's head, 61-62
    paper, 114
    papier-mâché, 63-68
        bottle people, 65-68
        character heads, 63-65
    round things, 70
    salt and starch, 114
    scrapwood animals, 61-63
    totem poles, 76-78
Sea, 161-163
Seasonal styrofoam prints, 50-52
Seasons, 113
Self-portraits, 167-168
Shadows, 192-194
Shapes:
    attached with paper spring, 152
    cylindrical, 17
    free-form, 152
    geometric, 114
    importance, 15
    repeated, 89-90
    round, 26, 70-72
    starters, 151-152
    three-dimensional effect, 152
    two funny ones, 152
Shields, Indian, 81-83
Showers, sudden, 209-211
Silhouette prints, stencil, 56-58
Size, creating depth, 85-87
Skills, art, 113-115
Sky, watercolor, 97-99
Sounds, 183-184
Space, 85-87
Speech, 117
Speeding, 208-209
Sponge, tempera and, 35-37
Stained glass:
    tissue, 91
    watercolors, 101-104
        black crayon drawing, 104
        bright colors, 102
        curved arch, 104
        decorative colored shapes, 103
        displaying, 104
        drawing kept simple, 104
        each different, 103, 104
        each shape different color, 104

Stained glass *(cont.)*
   watercolors *(cont.)*
      frame contour, 104
      large center picture, 104
      lead work, 102
      one color at time, 104
      personal interests, 102, 104
      pointed arch, 104
      round picture in circle, 104
      shapes of windows, 102-104
      story or design, 102
Stencil silhouette prints, 56-58
Stick painting, 33-35
Still life:
   drawing, 26-27
   wallpaper, 87-89
Stocking hand puppets:
   attaching parts, 123
   creatures possible, 122
   eyes, 122
   language arts, 123
   manes or hair, 123
   mouths that move, 122
   needles, crochet hooks, 121
   present plays, 123
   raid rag bag, 121
   sewing, 123
   teeth, 122
   tongue, 122
Storybook puppets, 126-128
Straws, blowing tempera, 31
String and oak tag, print, 52-54
Stuffed storybook puppets:
   character, 126-127
   cloth or yarn scraps, 128
   crayons, 128
   drawing, 127
   features, 128
   front and back, 127
   full skirt, 127
   handle, 128
   large, 128
   long, thin parts, 127
   newspaper stuffing, 127, 128
   oral book reports, 128
   plump enough to stuff, 127
   six inch opening, 127-128
   staplers, 127
   unique details, 127
   wide sleeves or legs, 127
Styrofoam prints, 50-52
Sunset or sunrise, 97

T

Taste, terrific, 204-206
Tempera:
   blizzard, picture, 197-199
   blowing, 31-33
   cardboard carton creatures, 72-74
   Christmas cards, 52-54
   color mixing, 37-38
   drawing gestures, 22
   egg cartons, 113-114
   emphasis on detail, 40-42
   large brushes, 38-40
   leaf prints, 45-47
   oak tag prints, 54-56
   paper cups, 114
   papier-mâché heads, 63-65
   portraits, 42-44
   potato prints, 47-50
   printing projects, 114
   sponge, 35-37
   stencil silhouette prints, 56-58
   stick painting, 33-35
   sudden shower, picture, 209-211
Texture:
   drawings, 24-26
   rubbings, 186-188
Tissue paper:
   prints, 58-60
   transparent windows, 90-93
Topics, 113
Torn paper scenes, 79-81
Totem poles, 76-78
Transparent tissue windows, 90-93
Tree, 190-192

U

Undersea excursions, 161-163
Unity, 89-90

V

Visages, collage, 146-148

W

Wallpaper:
   potato print, 50
   still lifes, 87-89

Index

Watercolor:
    out at night, 100-101
    painting from life, 110-111
    portraits, 105-107
    sky, 97-99
    stained glass windows, 101-104
    storybook people, 105-107
    sunset or sunrise, 97
    wash, 97-99
        blue of sky, 98
        broad area of color, 97
        clouds, 98
        frustration avoided, 99
        long sweeps of brush, 99
        silhouette added, 99
        start at top of paper, 98
        sunset, 99
        "wash," term, 97
    wax resist, 100-101
    wet paper, rain forest, 107-109
        blotting, 109
        colors found, 108
        demonstrate, 108
        details, 109
        large brush first, 109

Watercolor *(cont.)*
    wet paper, rain forest *(cont.)*
        light colors, 108
        no puddles, 109
        sky and sun, 108
        spreading and running, 109
        tree trunks, 108
        types of plants, 108
        water over entire paper, 108
Wax resist:
    aquarium pictures, 173-174
    paintings, 100-101
Weeds, 181-183
Wet paper, working on, 107-109
Wind, looking at, 184-186
Windows:
    transparent tissue, 90-93
    watercolors, 101-104
Wood, scrap, 61-63
Wrapping paper, 50

Z

Zoo animals:
    cartons, 72-74
    torn paper, 79-81